GOD IN THE CONVERSATION

by John F. Smed

Published by Prayer Current

God in the Conversation

Introduction

"We need to talk."

I know what that means. Our life is getting too busy. We have no time for each other. My wife Caron and I need face-to-face communication.

Today, life is too busy for most of us. We inhabit the social, entertainment and consumer media we make. Swept up by a myriad of images, we are caught in a tide. We are numbed into silence by an overwhelming flow of 'luminescent newness.' Shiny wave after shiny wave cascades over us. It's all we can do to clamor to our feet and wait for the next wave to hit.

As wave after wave breaks, we tumble in the surf. We lose sight of each other. We text. We chat. We Facebook. We struggle to relate. We are 'together alone.'

"We need to talk."

***

We need God in the conversation

In our back yard is an 800 year-old Douglas fir tree (so we were told by a horticulturist). It is some 30 meters high and more than 4 meters around. It grew from a seed smaller than a grain of wheat.

Meaningful conversations are the small seeds that grow large in understanding and friendship. Small conversations have potential for great growth.

When we talk about God we dig deep, reach high, and range far. Questions about God lead to all great questions: "Why am I here?" "Where do I fit?" "Where am I going?"

The human soul has almost unlimited capacity for growth. Sow God into the conversation, and water this seed in prayer – hope, faith, and love will take root, grow up, and spread out. It could be unstoppable.

A note about these conversations

Each conversation in this book is fresh in my mind. Most of them have been within a few years of this writing. I have done my best to narrate the details of our conversation and to avoid dramatic embellishment. Conversations vary in length. They tend to be longer and go deeper as the book progresses.

It will be obvious that I come to these interactions with Christian faith. Those I discuss with have a wide range of different beliefs. I converse with a variety of spiritual seekers – Sikh, Muslim, atheist, agnostic, nominal, and 'church burned.' Conversations take place in a variety of settings – on a plane ride, in a taxi, on a treadmill, picking up a hitchhiker, smoking a cigar, after a golf match, and a few on their death bed. In every situation, what each person believes matters to them. What they believe matters to me. These are some of my most interesting and rewarding conversations.

PART 1:
DIVING IN:
Conversations About God and Other Gods

God in the Conversation

A Temple in a Taxi

We arrive at Winnipeg International Airport. We are headed to a conference. It's the middle of winter – early morning and bitterly cold. Winter and cold are synonymous in Winnipeg. Affectionately referred to as 'Winterpeg' – this place is known for 'nine months winter and three months tough sleddin.'" We stand in line waiting for a taxi. In sixty seconds, fingers numb. When high wind speed and very low temperatures merge news bulletins warn people to stay home. I mean, 'baby, it's cold outside.'

Winnipeg,
Manitoba,
Canada

The line is short. A cab pulls up and we dive in. The cab is toasty warm. We settle in for the thirty minute ride to the hotel and convention center.

The driver wears a turban – so I know he is Sikh. Spot a taxi pretty much anywhere in Canada and there is a good chance you'll have a Sikh driver. They hail from the Punjab province of India. I've experienced their cheerful friendliness on numerous occasions. You get in a cab and they make you feel welcome. Call it hospitality.

They love Canada and are proud of their new country. Canada seems to have an open door policy for their immigration. They adopt our sports with the same enthusiasm they adopt our country. They make rabid hockey fans.

I find it easy to strike up a conversation with Sikh people – especially about prayer. They seem to love discussing their religion.

Most devout Sikhs go to the temple each morning if they can, but some will tune into satellite.

Once we are seated, settled and warm, we exchange greetings. "Good morning, Sirs." He asks if we had a nice trip. I ask if business is good.

A few minutes later I bring up a topic of common interest. We are off and running.

"Do you mind me asking, 'Are you Sikh?'"

"Yes, I am sir."

"So did you have a chance to say your prayers this morning?"

Cheerfully he replies, "Yes. I said my prayers at six. I do so each day."

"Did you go to temple or did you listen to satellite?"

"Oh, I go to temple each morning before work. I also go at the end of the day."

Prayer is at the heart of Sikh worship.

***

Sikhism is true to its eastern origins. It is pantheistic but combines this with monotheistic ideas. Sikhs worship Ultimate reality as one, yet they speak of the creator and address this ultimate reality in a personal way.

They have a deep reverence for their teachers – gurus. They try to be understanding of other religions. Counter to Hinduism, they worship God in abstract form, and don't use images or statues to help them. Sikh worship can be public or private. Sikhs can pray at any time and any place.

The Sikh code of conduct lays down a stern discipline for the start of the day. There are set prayers in the morning, evening, and before going to sleep. A Sikh aims to get up early, bathe, and then start the day by meditating on God.

For the Sikh believer, God is beyond description. They feel able to pray to God as a person and a friend who cares for them. Many Sikhs regard prayer as a way of spending time in company with God.

True to their eastern roots, for prayer to be really effective a person tries to empty himself of everything of this world so that he or she can perceive God.

Although Sikhs can worship on their own, they see congregational worship as having its own special merits. They believe that God is visible in the Sikh congregation or Sangat, and that God is pleased by the act of serving the Sangat.

Congregational Sikh worship takes place in a place called a Gurdwara – a word combining 'guru' or teacher and 'dwara' meaning gateway. At the Gurdwara, through prayer the worshipper connects with the Guru Granth Sahib or most sacred scriptures of Sikhism.

An interesting note – Sikh public worship can be led by any Sikh, male or female, who is competent to do so. This might explains why Sikh women are often strong leaders and freely contribute to any discussion. One commentator elaborates:

> "The role of women in Sikhism is outlined in the Sikh scriptures. A woman is to be regarded as equal to the man. In Sikhism, women are considered to have the same souls as men and an equal right to grow spiritually. They are allowed to lead religious congregations, take part in the Akhand Path (the continuous recitation of the Holy Scriptures), perform Kirtan (congregational singing of hymns), work as a Granthi, and participate in all religious, cultural, social, and secular activities. As such, Sikhism was among the first major world religions to imply that women are equal to men. "Guru Nanak proclaimed the equality of men and women, and both he and the gurus that succeeded him allowed women to take a full part in all the activities of Sikh worship and practice."

***

Our taxi host is more than willing to continue the conversation. I can't recall a cold reply when I bring up the topic of prayer with someone who wears a turban. This is a stereotype, but a good one, and true to my experience.

One time my wife and I are visiting New York City. We take a cab. We are halfway into the city and in the middle of a good conversation. I find out our driver goes to temple each day.

"Why do you say your prayers each day?" I ask.

He glances and points to the right. He asks, "Do you see these people?" We are headed down the east side of Central Park. The sidewalk is crowded.

"Yes. I do."

Animated, he says, "If I did not say my prayers, I do not see anyone. When I pray I see people."

I'm impressed. "Wow! Now that's a good answer – and a good reason to pray."

***

Back to the cold morning in Winnipeg. Connan pipes in. "I am a Christian and prayer is important to me as well." He adds, "I love to pray each day wherever I am – and to speak with God at the beginning and the end of my day."

Our driver says, "Yes. This is a good thing."

"In fact, I can say my prayers here and now in this taxi because God is here too."

He agrees, "God is everywhere."

While they're talking a new insight hits me. Call it a revelation. I put what the driver is saying and what Connan is saying together – and come up with a third idea.

I speak up. "Praying anywhere is wonderful. May I tell you something even more amazing? This may surprise you."

I pause for a few seconds. I am still processing my insight. New discoveries take time to form. Revelations need to be savored before we speak them.

"I just realized something as you two were talking about prayer."

Connan turns to look at me. Our host looks in the rear view mirror.

I come out a say it. "I do not have to go to temple to pray. I am a temple!"

In the mirror I see a quizzical look, as if to ask, "What do you mean?"

"I believe God is in me and that I am in God. I am always in the place of prayer because I am always in the presence of God. The Bible tells us that if we believe in God's son, Jesus, we become a temple of prayer for God."

***

This 'temple-within' idea is birthed from a rich complex of scripture. The Bible teaches that Jesus resides in the heart of anyone who puts their faith in him: In John 17 Jesus prays, and asks the father,

> "...that they may all be one, just as you, Father, are in me, and I in you, that they also may be in us, ...I in them and you in me, that they may become perfectly one,...Father, I desire that they also, whom you have given me, may be with me where I am, to see my glory."

Getting to know God is like entering a banquet hall with him as host and the believer as permanent guest:

> "Behold, I stand at the door and knock. If anyone hears my voice and opens the door, I will come in to him and eat with him, and he with me." *(Revelation 3:7)*

Union with Christ is the essence of the Christian faith – *"Christ in you, the hope of glory." (Colossians 1:27)* This makes each believer a temple – who is always in the presence of God. *"Or do you not know that your body is a temple of the Holy Spirit within you, whom you have from God?" (1 Corinthians 6:19)*

***

I try to explain several ideas in a few sentences. "I can always pray anywhere, anytime because, like every believer I always have access to God. I am always in the presence of God! He actually says that I am a temple of the Spirit of God."

I am not sure how our driver receives this idea. I know I am excited. It takes my breath away.

We pull up to the hotel. It's around the corner from the convention center, only a few steps through bitter cold.

Smiles all around, we are thankful for the ride – and even more thankful for the warm conversation. Our driver has been a gracious host. He has given of himself. He has shared what most matters to him.

This conversation has been special. Because of a real interest in each other's experience of prayer – I learn something new and important about my own prayers.

I come to realize, "I am a temple in a taxi."

God in the Conversation

Is God by Any Name Still God?

Each one of us has a name. As we grow through life our name becomes a key part of our identity.

How people speak our name matters. It is important to have a 'good name.'

God has a name. It is part of his identity. It matters to him who he is. It matters how we speak his name.

At the burning bush Moses asks God his name. God replies, "I am who I am." This is interesting – and enigmatic. God is telling Moses – 'I am beyond any name you can give me. I am who I am – eternally and unchangeably God.' We don't give God a name. We are not qualified. Only God can name God.

God defines himself. He fills the name 'God' with rich meaning. Another time Moses asks God to reveal himself. God does this by speaking his name and giving it meaning:

*The Lord passed before Moses and proclaimed the
name of the Lord, 'the Lord, the Lord, a God merciful
and gracious, slow to anger, and abounding is
steadfast love and faithfulness.' (Exodus 34:6)*

God's name means a ton. His name describes who
he is. 'God' means mercy, grace, patience, love, and
faithfulness.

My name is part of me. How others treat my name
matters to me. If someone misuses my name or
misrepresents me, I can get a bad name. For example,
someone says, "John can't be counted on. He is
undependable." If this is untrue, my name has been
discredited. I am justly offended. I want my name upheld.

The same is true of God, only infinitely more. God
is not just any god. God's name is part of him. God is
jealous about his name. He wants us to speak his name
with reverence and love, *"Do not take the name of the
Lord your God in vain." (Exodus 20:4)*

***

Some years ago, when we lived in Atlanta, I had an
interesting conversation on the topic of God's name.

I am working at a Methodist conference center. We often
use it for training events. Over time, I get to know one of
the elderly women who runs the snack and soda kiosk.

Margaret is friendly and witty. We talk every day.
Sometimes we just chide each other. She likes that.
Other times we have a spiritual conversation. Margaret
has lots of good questions about God and faith

One day I greet her, "Margaret, how are you doing today?"

After we chat for a while, the topic turns to prayer.

Margaret asks, "When someone prays does it really
matter what they call God? Aren't all prayers accepted
by God no matter what name we use?"

It's not the first time I've heard this. Many believe that God by any other name is still God. 'God,' 'Allah,' 'Krishna,' 'Ground of Being,' 'Higher Power' – any name will do.

I decide to explore. "Why do you believe it doesn't matter what we call God?"

"I believe God hears anyone who prays to him, from any religion. It's not just Christians that God listens to. I can't believe some people have their prayers answered and not others. God hears everyone. The name we call God doesn't matter."

"Hmm. Let me think about that." I don't say anything at the time. I take this thought home and think over what she says.

I imagine Margaret is thinking about being fair and open to other religions when she says that what we call God is a matter of indifference. She looks at things from the viewpoint of our common humanity. She believes this is a bigger and better perspective than assuming one religion is right.

I make a decision to turn the conversation around – look at things from God's viewpoint.

The next morning, arriving at the retreat center, I pass by Margaret and say, "Hi Sandy. Beautiful day isn't it? How are you today?"

She turns to me with a puzzled look. "You know that's not my name." She sounds a bit miffed. "What do you mean, Sandy? My name is Margaret. You know that. I don't know who Sandy is."

"Why does it matter what name I use?"

"It matters to me."

"Thank you Margaret. I just wanted to reply to your point about God. I've been thinking over what you said yesterday. Remember you asked, 'Does it matter what name we call God?' I believe it does."

Margaret has calmed down. "Okay. Go ahead. Tell me what you're thinking."

"God doesn't go by just any name. God has an identity. He's not human, but he is personal. His name reveals who he is. It matters to him what we call him – just like it matters to you. "

"When I called you by the wrong name you got upset. Why is that?"

Margaret thinks a few seconds, "Okay, I see what you mean. It's strange to be called by the wrong name – especially by someone you know."

"Yes, if I call you by the wrong name – it means I really don't know you very well. It's like I have forgotten you. Like you don't matter to me. It's the same with God. Call him by the wrong name and he is upset. It means we don't really know him. It means we have forgotten who he is. It means God doesn't really matter."

She takes a minute to think about it. She gives a friendly smile. "Okay John. That's clever. I get what you are saying."

Over time, I have other interesting conversations with Margaret. This one is the most memorable.
This time we break through formalities and jokes.

We move from the head to the heart. I have a chance to share my faith in God with her. I get to hear her heart and soul. We're both richer for it. We're better friends too.

A Papa Prays for His Children

He is earnest. "How do you pray? How should I pray for my children?"

This young man is Muslim.

Our conversation starts earlier. I am reading a book. We are moving five hundred miles an hour at thirty five thousand feet. Apparently, this heavenward experience frees some people to talk about God.
He is gazing out the window. I notice he is young – so young I'm surprised when he tells me he is married and has two young children.

He glances over and asks what I am reading.

I tell him I am reading a book on prayer. "I want to dive in and go deeper in my prayer life."

He smiles, "I do as well."

He is curious. So am I.

"May I ask you a question? Can you tell me, what the difference is between prayer and meditation?"

He ponders for a moment. "I'm not sure. I know what prayer is but am not sure about meditation. What do you mean by meditation?"

"It seems to me that meditation takes us inside. It's an attempt to connect with one's self. On the other hand, prayer is directed upward and is an attempt to connect with God."

"Yes. I see what you mean. That makes sense. "

I ask him, "Do you pray?"
"Oh yes, I pray to God every day as part of my religion. It is very important to me."

"Are you Muslim?"

"Yes, I am."

"Do you observe Ramadan?"

"I am not strict in this."

Ramadan is the ninth month of the Muslim year, during which strict fasting is observed from sunrise to sunset. It derives from Arabic Ramadan, from ramada 'be hot.' Ramadan can occur in any season; originally it was in one of the hot months.

I ask, "When you pray, what do you ask God for?"

"I pray for my children. I love them deeply. I want to be able to teach them how to live well. I pray they will believe in God and enjoy the life he has given us."

Our conversation turns to parenting and family life. We discuss the challenges of raising children today. His two children are not yet in school. We agree it is a tough time to raise kids. The challenges are real for those who believe in God. How can we help our children understand our beliefs in the current craziness of the internet, social media, advertising, and the avalanche of secular beliefs? It's not easy to guide them into a life of purpose and dignity.

"Yes," the young man says, "This is a very great concern to me. I want my children to have rea hope –

more than prosperity. I am very concerned about this. I pray about it all the time."

His openness is refreshing.

I tell him, "My wife and I have raised five children. We have grandkids. I understand and very much agree with your concern. I admire your love for your children. I am encouraged to see a father so very prayerful."

At this point an announcement comes over the PA. "We are beginning our descent into Vancouver." He ignores this and continues the conversation.

His eyes are lit with intensity. "Please tell me how you pray. I want to learn how to pray better – especially for my children."

What a great question. What a privilege to be asked.

I take a long minute to think before replying.

"I am pretty sure I pray for the same things you do – for my children and grandchildren. I want them to grow up with faith in God and to live a life of purpose. I don't want them just to be successful so they can have more than others. I pray for them to have a loving heart towards God and towards others."

I add, "There is only one significant difference between my prayer and yours."

"What is that? Please tell me."

"When I pray I always pray in the name of Jesus."

He's not offended. Muslims have a great deal of respect for Jesus. His eyes are wide open. He wants me to continue.

"The Old Testament prophets teach that God is infinitely holy. I know you also believe this. I realize God is holy and I am not. I can never approach God on my own merit. I can't just run into his presence with my prayers.

The problem is deep. No matter how hard I try –
no matter how much I pray or how much good I do, I
cannot make myself worthy to approach God. One of the
prophets speaks these words from God, *"Who would dare
of himself to approach me?"* (Jeremiah 30:31)

"I believe Jesus makes it possible for me to pray.
He died on the cross to bring me to God. He wins me
forgiveness of sins. He invites me to pray. Now I freely
come into the presence of God. I trust in Jesus and come
in his name."

This young father takes it all in. I'm sure he
understands. He is Muslim so I don't need to explain
concepts of holiness and forgiveness. He has a far off
look. He is going inside – taking time to think this over.

Wheels touch down and we taxi to the gate.

He comes out of his thoughts, and turns to me
with a smile, "Thank you. I am very glad we had this
conversation. Thank you for sharing these things
with me."

"I feel the same way. It has been a blessing to
meet you."

I add the Muslim sentiment, "God has meant it to be."

Our Path to God or God's Path to Us

"I am the path." ~Jesus (John 14:6)

I am winding my way through the Fraser River Valley. It's a mild day – the sun finds its way through the clouds. The surrounding mountains are majestic, bearded with a full growth of fir. Above the tree line are sharp, sculpted, granite peaks – crevasses billowed with permanent snow.

Alongside we have a full vista of the mighty Fraser River. This river travels 1375 kilometers, carving deep paths through granite. Explorers like Simon Fraser made their way to the coast along this river. Varieties of spawning salmon fill this river at different times of the year. Deep below, huge sturgeon fish glide slowly and effortlessly. They weigh up to 1100 pounds and live up to 150 years. The river widens to 200 meters at some points and narrows to 20 meters at canyons like

"Hells' Gate." Aptly named, at this point, all hell breaks loose. No one gets through these rapids. There's no way to forge and there is no way to portage. First peoples and explorers used ropes to rappel through the steep canyon walls.

As I pass the river I notice a weathered hitchhiker. He wears a lumberjack toque. Miles from nowhere he is thumbing his way to who knows where. Most times, I just drive by, but he catches my eye. He is older than most hitch hikers – perhaps 60. He is lean, muscular, and neatly dressed – a T-shirt, jeans, plaid jacket and tan work boots. He must work hard to stay in chiseled shape.

I pull over and signal him to come aboard. He sprints to the car, opens the door, and throws his knapsack in the back seat. He smiles a cheerful smile, "Thanks for the lift."

"No problem. Glad to help out."

His eyes are friendly and curious. They hint at inner intelligence. A smile naturally graces his face. Right away you know it's easy to like this guy. I do.

I find out his name is Ivan. He has a pronounced but pleasant accent. I think it's Slavic. "I am very glad you picked me up. I have an appointment with my boss down the road. I am almost late." It turns out Ivan is a handyman. He migrates up and down the B.C. Coast finding work along the way.

Conversation is easy. I discover he is conversational – and a philosopher.

Surrounded by the mountain splendor, I offer, "You have to feel good on a day like this. Makes a person want to be thankful."

Ivan responds, "Yes. Beauty like this makes a man happy."

Before long we are in a full and free current of thoughts and words.

Ivan dives in. He looks out the window and says, "If we open our eyes to nature and the world, we will realize that there is an essential oneness of all being." His tone expresses genuine wonder.

"Tell me what you mean."

"It is only our ego and selfish perspective that divides us. We think about differences too much. We divide and separate ourselves from the oneness we share with all things. Out here you can feel it."

I get what he is saying, but want to ask a question. "I agree we are one with all things. Aren't we also different from the rest of creation? Aren't we also individuals?"

He replies, "Every spiritual insight I have received leads me to believe that needless and harmful conflict in life comes from ego differentiation. We want our individuality, we fill our selfish needs – to the detriment of self and others." Ivan alludes to various seminars, retreats, workshops and teachers that have helped him along the way.

I listen to what he says – and how he says it. For Ivan good and evil are more than a theory.

"I agree. Nothing could be clearer. We all try to put self at the center. None of us is content to be equal. A selfish and uncontrolled ego explains a lot of the mayhem in the world."

"Yes. This is what I believe."

"Still, I have to say I'm rather fond of my self. I accept the unity of all things but I'm not eager to give up the idea of being an individual. Could it be possible we are both one with the creation and at the same time individual?"

"Tell me what you mean."

"I am myself. You are yourself. To be an individual with a unique identity is a treasured part of life."

Ivan takes a minute to think this over. "Yes. I hear what you are saying."

He continues, "Let me explain. Take, for example, the different streams of religion and spiritual teaching. Each path provides valuable and helpful insights, but ultimately disagreements overwhelm the good. All paths of those who seek God, lead to the same place – if we can only see it. Common ground is more profound and important than differences. God is bigger than any one religion can conceive him."

At this point our conversation narrows. We enter some rapids.

I ask, "How do you know that all paths lead to God? How can you be confident that each religion holds only a part of the truth?"

"I have studied and thought about this for a long time."

"Okay," I say, "But wouldn't you need to know the 'whole truth' in order to know that each religion has only a part of it? You say all paths lead to God. Wouldn't someone need to all about each of the paths to know this? In fact wouldn't a person need to know what God thinks to say that every path leads to him?"

"I did not say I knew the whole truth, only that everyone knows a part of the truth."

I continue with my question. "I wonder if what you say is logical. I would think to say 'all paths lead to God' is something only God can say. Only God has access to the whole truth. Only God can tell how much of the whole truth someone knows. He alone knows which path leads to the truth."

Ivan is silent – pondering what I say.

***

It's a good time to take a breather. Alongside is a full vista of the mighty river. I slow a bit to take in the view. I tell Ivan about the greatness of the Fraser, the monster sturgeon, spawning salmon – and about the maelstrom upstream – Hell's Gate canyon. Surveying the majesty, we share a sense of awe.

After a while we resume our conversation. We go deeper.

I ask another question.

"You seem to say that each religion falls short. At the same time you say that each religion is equally valid because all paths lead to God. What about the great differences in belief? I know you don't mean to say that the 'jihad' of Mohammed and 'turn the other cheek' of Jesus are equally valid."

Quickly, he replies, "No, of course not. The teachings of Jesus are different. I did not say every path is the same as the others – certainly not when it comes to war. This is a misinterpretation of their religion."

"I ask the question for a reason. With all the complexities of different faiths, how can you be sure that no religion, no philosopher or no teacher has the right path – or at least a better path than others?"

Ivan counters, "It's not a matter of logic. You have to discover this yourself. Every religion seeks the same God by its own path."

"You believe that all paths move towards the truth. If we all would agree on this, we could find peace between the religions."

"Yes. I very much believe this."

"I have another problem. Surprisingly few religious people agree with you. Muslims, Jews, Christians, and even many Hindus and Buddhists believe they have the right teaching about God. This is more than half the world. People of different religious convictions are willing to suffer and even be martyred for what they believe. In fact, as a Christian I believe I am on the right path."

"I understand that."

"It seems to me, if I am being exclusive in my claim to know the truth, you are as well. I say I am on the right path. Others are mistaken. You say all paths lead to the truth. Those who do not believe this may be well intentioned – but they are mistaken. Like me, you are making an exclusive claim. You exclude those people who to claim to know the truth and have the right path. This includes all those who do not agree that all paths lead to God."

It's Ivan's turn to make his points and to question me.

"But isn't it sheer arrogance for any human being to argue their path is the only right path? By what reasoning can someone claim to have the right path and maintain that other paths are simply off course? Isn't this disrespectful of other religions?"

I agree with him. When it comes to claims 'to know' we have to be humble. We are finite and our reasoning is flawed. Each person knows so little. We are easily deceived and mislead. The human mind is a leaky sieve, a hodgepodge of ideas, quick to jump to conclusions, more defensive of self than truth. Aren't all dogmatic claims to the truth, by definition, simply pride of or ego?

At the same time, I am frustrated. Within, something or someone is nagging.

I stop to listen to this inner prompting. Suddenly a spark is triggered. A light goes on. I have a revelation. Revelation literally means 'pull back the veil.' The veil is removed. I hit upon an undeniable and solid truth.

My mind fills with a rapid tumble of thoughts.
I navigate the turbulence and try to find words to
express my insight. A minute later, things become clear.
I go with Ivan's argument.

"I have to agree with you. Any human claim to know
the right path towards God is arrogant. We could never
have enough knowledge to eliminate the other paths
to God."

Ivan's eyes tell me he's glad I affirm his concern.

"But let me ask you. Is it not possible that God has
a path to man?"

He is curious where I am going.

I'm excited. Words pour out, "Have you considered
an alternative – a path from God to man? What if
God has carved a path to us? What if God levels the
mountains and raises the valleys and makes his own
path to mankind? What if God reveals this path to us
through his chosen prophets and teachers?"

"Hmm. Interesting. Keep going."

"If God makes a path to us, there can be one path to
God. It's not a path made by human religions. It's a path
God reveals. If there is this 'God path,' the concerns
about being exclusive and arrogant disappear. A
believer would be on the right path because he accepts
the one path provided by God."

"I think I understand."

"In fact, this is what I believe. The search for truth
is not about finding our way to God. It's about God
finding his way to us. It is not so much a path to God –
it is God's path to us."

"I admit, this is a new thought. I have not heard this
before."

"Isn't it interesting, in the gospel, Jesus says,
'I am the path, no one comes to the father except by me.'
(John 14:6). Jesus makes a path from God to us when he
is born. Jesus makes a way to God when he gives his life
to forgive our sins. That's why Jesus is the path. If we
accept him – we have a path to God."

We come to Ivan's exit. His place of work is just
around the bend. I can just drop him off at the top of
the exit. Instead I ask, "How far down the road?"

"Not far, just a kilometer or two. Just drop me off at
the top."

"Let me drive you."

I take him the rest of the way.

When we arrive at his place of work, Ivan opens
the door, and gives me his winning smile. He takes
my hand with a warm, friendly grip. "Thank you for
the ride. This has been special. And thank you for the
excellent conversation."

"Thank you Ivan. I enjoyed meeting you. I really
found our discussion valuable. I learned some new
things from our talk. I hope we meet again."

As I drive back to the highway I feel good. I enjoy
that I met Ivan. I like him. The foundations of my
beliefs have not altered, but I have learned a lot. I have
a respect for Ivan's ideas because I appreciate the man.
He's a man of sincerity and substance – worth listening
to. The conversation was short but deep and fast
moving. The door of friendship quickly opened.

I realize when Jesus says, "I am the path," he makes a
bold claim. It is obviously an exclusive claim. No other
spiritual or religious leader or philosopher has dared to
say this – not even remotely. However, Jesus' claim is an

offer. It is also universal. The path is wide enough for every one who wants to follow it. No one is excluded from the offer.

We need a path to God. We can't find our way through the turbulent streams of life. We're thrown every which way and lose our bearings. God has to find us. He has to make a way. God plunges into the narrow canyon of our troubled waters. He dives in. He rescues us.

Confused by Too Many Gods

When it comes to finding a religion people get confused. There are too many options. Religions seem to run in every direction. There is pantheism, New Age, Dalai Lama, agnosticism and atheism – as well as the major world religions. Christianity is divided between Catholics and Protestants – and a hundred varieties between the two. Without a road map, religions diverge and merge, ending up in an undifferentiated tangle.

I recall a conversation with Teri. My wife and I meet Teri through an online AirBnB booking. We stay in her home. I am waiting in the entryway for Caron. I can see Teri in the kitchen, feeding her little girl. We get talking. She is curious about what I do.

"I work with people to help them find God – sometimes in the church, sometimes not."

Teri tells me, "I had a Catholic upbringing. I even became an acolyte. Then I went to university and heard that Christianity is just one religion among many. They taught me that all the myths of Christianity, like the incarnation and resurrection, are common to other religions."

"That really challenged your Catholic background."

"Yeah. I couldn't go back to what I used to believe. I tried experimenting with other philosophies. I studied other religions. I got into meditation for a while. For some reason nothing hit home. Pretty soon I was just confused."

"So going to church was no longer an option for you?"

"No. Not any more."

Teri is concerned about the 'public face' of religion. "When I look at fundamentalism, I really have a problem. Everyone thinks they have the inside track. Everyone else is wrong."

"It sounds like a hard place. You look at all the different ideas and you get confused. You think of choosing one faith and you worry about fundamentalism. Where does that leave you?"

"I'm not sure. I can't see how we can make it through life without something to believe. I'm happy for prosperity and the benefits of western society but wonder where we're headed. I admit I'm anxious about a world driven by science and technology."

She adds, "My husband is avid that scientific progress is the key to the future. I don't agree. We used to argue about it. We'd both get upset. I don't want to argue anymore, so now I just drop the conversation." She sighs. I feel her resignation.

Teri is powerless to believe. She can't go back to her
old faith. She can't accept a modern secular view.
At the same time she can't be whole hearted about other
approaches. She is stuck in the middle of nowhere.
The search for truth is just too much to deal with.

I have met others like Teri. I am pretty sure there
are many.

"I can hear your frustration. It sounds painful.
Do you have any kind of spiritual practice?"

"I meditate when things get hard."

I think I can help. I came out of an incoherent bird's
nest of beliefs before God found me. I offer up a silent
prayer, looking for wisdom.

After some silence, I decide to share something.
"When I get confused or overwhelmed, I just pray.
I know I can't think my way to God. Prayer connects me
with God and helps put things together."

Teri looks interested, but hesitant. "I can't say
that I pray. Sometimes I meditate."

In my satchel, I have a book about prayer. I take it
out and offer it to her. "Do you think you might be
interested in the prayer life of Jesus?"

I can tell by her look, she isn't ready. Still, she accepts
the book, "My mom will like this."

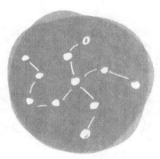

PART 2:

CHALLENGED:

Conversations About God and No Gods

Confused by No Gods

Where some people hear noise, others hear a tune.
                              ~Michael Polanyi

Mike and Brenda are new neighbors. We are new to the community too. We want to make friends. We have them over for a BBQ. I find out pretty soon that Mike is an explorer of ideas. He welcomes a talk with God in the conversation.

He was raised Anglican. He believes in God, and says he prays to the Father, and to the Son, and to the Holy Spirit. This isn't the whole story.

This isn't the whole story. A year or so earlier, a friend encouraged Mike to read "The God Delusion" by Richard Dawkins. Dawkins argues that faith in God is a delusion. Religious beliefs are 'a misfiring of something useful...an accidental by-product of evolution.' Science deals with nothing but the facts. Religion conjures up imaginary forces and entities.

Mike read the book. It knocked the spiritual wind out of him.

Mike doesn't want to accept Dawkins' arguments or his mocking tone, but he doesn't have an answer. He admits, "Reading Dawkins shook my faith in God to the bones. I was knocked off my feet. For a long time I was in a daze. I wondered if there would be anything left to my faith."

***

For Dawkins and other atheists, evolution explains how everything works. Start to finish, big bang to frozen cosmos, biology or cosmology, nothing in the universe falls outside the laws of evolution. Random selection rules. There is no power above or within the cosmos beyond the simple blind processes of the physical world.

> "In a universe of blind physical forces and genetic replication...you won't find any rhyme or reason nor any justice...there is, at bottom, no design, no purpose, no evil and no good, nothing but blind pitiless indifference." ~Richard Dawkins, *River Out of Eden: A Darwinian View of Life*

Dawkins argues that mankind's only hope is to face the truths of science and get rid of the delusion. God is a dangerous delusion. Religious leaders use ideas about God to manipulate, control, and coerce people to do their bidding. Dawkins concludes that most of the violence and oppression in human history can be traced to those who believe in some kind of god.

***

I empathize with Mike. Who hasn't had their beliefs shaken?

"It sounds like your faith has been rocked. Where does that leave you?"

He shrugs. "I realized I still need my faith. I decided I didn't want to live life without God. I couldn't answer

Dawkins' arguments. I simply chose to live by faith in spite of what he said. I would rather live life with faith than without. I don't need to prove God to believe in him."

With visible regret he adds, "I have to admit I'm still disturbed by Dawkin's arguments."

Mike wants to believe. He also wants to know. He remembers the childhood of his faith – when believing in God seemed a natural thing.

I can tell that he has been wounded. It's unnerving when doubt threatens to take over.

I tell Mike, "I think I might be able to help."
"Really? Tell me."

"Dawkins has a problem. He doesn't pick on someone his own size. His arguments against God aren't strong or conclusive. He has been refuted – decisively I would say."

"Keep going."

"Dawkins assumes most scientists agrees with him. In fact a great many scientists believe in God. In a 2014 Religion in Science International study, only 38% of scientists believe there is a conflict between science and religion. BBC research in 2004 revealed that only 39% do not believe in God, 21% say they don't know.

Dawkins wants you to believe that every well-educated person agrees with him. In fact many of the best thinkers have squared off with his brand of atheism. G.K. Chesterton, Dorothy Sayers, and C.S. Lewis are great examples. More recently, a New York City pastor, Tim Keller, has written a book called *Reasons for God.* He challenges Dawkin's assumptions brilliantly.

A great many of us are more than satisfied these writers come out on top. Dawkins is aware of their arguments, but he doesn't represent them in his book."

I perk Mike's interest. He smiles, "That sounds significant."

I explain, "Let me share one of the counter-arguments. It's a standard defense of faith versus atheism. Have you heard about the discovery of DNA?"

"Sure."

"When Francis Crick and James Watson discovered the double helix and the workings of DNA, they were confident they had breached the hull of faith. They maintained the existence of God was no longer a necessary assumption.

Their argument was simple. We are made up of genes. Genes explain how life works. 'God created and designed life' has always been the explanation for how life works. With the discovery of DNA, they argued, "We no longer require the 'God hypothesis' to explain the design of life."

"They don't stop there. They go further and argue we don't need to believe in God to explain the origin of life. They say, "Life has been the unexplained mystery, which has always been explained by the 'God answer.' Now we know how life works and evolves, the riddle of life is explained. The mystery is solved. We no longer need to assume that God is the author of life."

Mike looks at me, "Well, what can you say to that?"

"A number of people challenge their argument. "Why is this logical?" they ask. "Just because you understand how something works – the cause and effects – doesn't mean you no longer need a Maker to explain how it came to be. Evolution might explain 'how things work.' It does not follow – 'there is therefore no need for God."

Defenders of the faith point out the obvious. "With the discovery DNA we have simply increased our awareness of the amazing complexity and beauty of life. We now know there is a dance going on in the molecular core of our being. If ever we needed an explanation for how life came to be – we need it now. The origin and design of our genes cries out for a maker or designer. Just because we know how a watch works does not mean we do not need a watchmaker."

I see the wheels turning. "I think I see what you are getting at."

"Mike, I assure you, for millions of people, belief in God is a matter of faith – but a faith that's reasonable. The infinite power, beauty, intricacy, and coherence of the universe cry out for a Creator. The world speaks about God. It points to God as the Creator. This idea is in the Bible:

> *For his invisible attributes, namely, his eternal power and divine nature, have been clearly perceived, ever since the creation of the world, in the things that have been made. So they are without excuse. (Romans 1:20)*

It is not just the design of the world that points to the architect. The entire universe in all its power, vastness and splendor, clearly reveals God as its maker. His Creator power originates and sustains everything. For all who have eyes to see, he is Creator and provider of all things.

****

Mike is smiling. "I like what you're saying. Thank you. Really. You've given my some hope. I want to read that book by Keller. I am going to re-examine my faith in God."

This is just the first of many God conversations I have with Mike. Mike reads Keller's *Reasons for God*. He rejoices in a solid refutation of atheism. We exchange other books and ideas. We start as neighbors. In time, we become good friends.

Seven Sins on a Treadmill

We are attending a workshop in downtown Toronto. I am up at first light to work out with a colleague in the hotel fitness center. Connan is on a treadmill two down from me. We engage in friendly banter.

A woman steps on the machine between us and starts her routine. It turns out she works for a city school board and is attending education meetings. Connan and I continue our conversation. Somehow we touch on the upcoming election.

She treads in and comments on the current conservative prime minister. "I just hate that Stephen Harper and his gang," she says. "They have to go."

I decide to reply. "Why?" I ask. "Surely, you don't want the other guys?"

I think I've hit a nerve. Pace quickening, pulse rising, she says, "They're out to destroy the environment. They don't do a thing about the tar sands. Big money and oil rule their decisions. They're going to ruin the world."

I get her point. According to the Pembina Institute, average greenhouse gas emissions for Alberta oil sands extraction and upgrading are estimated to be 3.2 to 4.5 times as intensive per barrel as for conventional crude oil. If Alberta were a country, at a rate of 69 tons CO_2 equivalent per person, its per capita greenhouse gas emissions would be higher than any other country in the world.

I venture a reply, "So do you think the environment is the key issue for the upcoming election?"

"Maybe it isn't the only issue. It's definitely the most important. We don't want the next generation to inherit a polluted world. Someone has to stop these guys. They just don't give a damn." She's exercised about this. Facing forward, body language tells me she's not open to debate.

I glance over at Connan. He shrugs his shoulders, "What can you say?" Connan is a good sport, always ready to discuss religion or politics, but he wonders if we haven't hit a dead end. I don't give up that easy. I figure our new exercise friend stepped into the conversation so she might be open to some friendly debate.

I try a new tack. I get an idea. A light goes on. I hope it's a prompting from God.

I take a calculated risk. I flip the question on its head.

"I agree the environment is important. Still I am pretty confident there are at least seven issues more important than the oil sands."

Connan finishes his run. He moves over to the weights. Quizzical, he looks at me, "Where are you going with this?"

She slows her pace and turns with a furrowed brow, "What are you talking about?" She looks credulous.

"Well you know – the seven things that have always been most important in any society – the heart of the whole thing."

Credulous, she says, "Go on."

For me it is 30 minutes, 3.5, kilometers and 300 calories later. I need to slow my pace and my pulse. I pause for a minute.

The break lets her ponder where I might be headed. It also provides a breather so the conversation can cool a bit.

I try to speak calmly and matter-of-factly. "Well it's the same old seven things. You know, the big ones – wrath, greed, envy, sloth, gluttony, lust, and pride. These seven vices are a lot more serious than issues of the environment."

Maybe she appreciates the creative turn of conversation. "Okay. Tell me what you're getting at."

"When it comes to change, we have to go inside before we fix what's outside. We have to address these seven inner vices before we deal with the outer destruction of the planet."

"Hmm."

I explain, "In the middle ages, travelling theatre troupes acted out the dangers of these sins. They would personify each one, and show how they need to be kept in check before they destroy the soul. It was a powerful message. This drama was the only entertainment most people had. Remember, there was no newspapers, computers, or televisions.

"The seven deadly sins represent the pollution of our collective heart – what's inside all of us. What's inside comes first. Oil sands projects explain how we wreck the environment; greed, envy, and gluttony go a long way to explaining why. The outside is the consequence of what's going on inside. You can never fix the outside unless you work on the inside."

Stepping off the treadmill, she looks me in the eye. It isn't a friendly look, but neither is it angry. She has cooled from overheated to lukewarm.

She counters, "You say that the inside is more important than the outside. Why does the inside come first? I still think that it is criminal to neglect the environment."

I explain, "They're called the seven deadly sins for a reason. The world we live in is important. If we neglect the environment we're in big trouble. On the other hand, if we neglect our soul we're dead.

"Politicians focus on outside issues for good reasons. The heart is harder to change than the environment. They want to tackle the outside issues and make them the big deal. We ignore the ecosystem of our heart and inner motive. We focus on externals in order to distract us from dealing with inside issues. We don't want to be wrong. We don't want to go inside. That means, the inner pollution never gets cleaned up. It just accumulates until the arteries of our spiritual heart are hopelessly clogged."

She ponders for a minute, then replies, "I have to admit that's an interesting perspective."

"A polluted environment is the result of a bunch of polluted hearts. You can't just tell people to start treating the world with respect. You can try to vote and legislate clean air and water into the world but it won't last. Clean up the heart, and you'll clean up the world."

She has cooled down. She doesn't say anything. I can tell she is pondering what I am saying. She could be looking at her own heart.

I decide to go deeper. "Jesus says something interesting to the politicians of his time, "You always clean the outside of the cup and neglect the inside.' Then he tells them, 'First clean the inside of the cup, and then clean the outside.'

We step off the treadmill within a few minutes of each other, me first.

We finish our exercise and our conversation at the same time. We have had a good workout in more ways than one.

She has a smile. "I have to admit, you have an interesting perspective."

Cool down period is over. So is our talk.

Up in Smoke

He's a smoker. He's also 'church-burned.' We get to know each other over these common interests – smoke and church.

Caron and I are on vacation in Hawaii. We are forty years, five children, and ten grandchildren into marriage.

It's early evening. I grab a good book, a cigar, and head to the designed smoking area of the resort. I am sitting on a comfy bench, pulling on my cigar and reading an essay on the expansion of Christianity.

A big friendly looking guy sidles up and lights a cigarette. At first, I ignore him. I am into the article and into my cigar.

After a few minutes, I look up. We exchange greetings and talk about the weather. Later, I find out his name is Grant. He grew up in church. Somewhere this went up in smoke.

I notice Grant glancing at the book I'm reading.

"Want to know what I am reading?"

"Yeah, that's a huge book. I noticed the fine print."

He leans forward, inviting conversation.

"It's about a thousand pages, but it's interesting. I find it inspirational."

"Yeah. That's a lot. I read some, but not that much."

I show him the book. It's titled Perspectives in World Mission. I explain the book in a nutshell to Grant.

"It's a history about how Christianity expanded around the world – especially since 1850. Everything stays in Europe when the clergy is in charge. When the average person gets involved a lot starts happening. Things really start to grow."

"That sounds interesting," he responds.

***

The book is a fascinating historical study about the global spread of Christianity. The writer explains three phases of Christian expansion. First, when clergy and church structures hold the reins, advance is slow. Next, when everyday people get involved, things speed up and grow. The third stage is exponential growth. This occurs only when indigenous peoples take over and share their lives and the good news with their neighbors.

The move from clergy-led to people-led occurs around 1850, with the formation of mission societies. Up to this point there is little for the average Christian to do. Single women aren't allowed to become missionaries. A man named Hudson Taylor turns the thing on its head. He encourages everyone to get involved. In a short time, hundreds of mission societies form. Everyday Christians take the lead. They get involved in prayer, giving, and sending.

To fund the work, mission societies begin 'penny-a-week' giving. Society members bring a penny a week to help the cause. Even the poor can be an essential part of things.

Mission bulletins and magazines outline opportunities and describe needs around the world. Thousands read these updates. Reporting includes many heart-breaking stories of suffering, exploitation and poverty around the world. Something great comes out of this – an outpouring of compassion for the downtrodden. Readers start to lobby politicians to do something. The mission society becomes a powerful political and social force.

Women leap at the opportunity to serve the world. They form women's mission societies and begin recruiting, funding, and sending women overseas – eventually hundreds. One of these early missionaries is a fiery Irish teen, Amy Carmichael. She starts working with women factory workers in Ireland. They live in poverty and are often exploited. They have no protection and are often molested. Amy's passion and joy are infectious. The girls flock to her meetings. Many discover Jesus to be their help and protector. Several of the rescued women are enlisted to help.

Later Amy is sent to India. She spends the rest of her life in India saving little girls who are being trafficked into prostitution. In spite of opposition from collaborators, this work thrives. There is a secret to her success – she recruits fellow workers from among the ones she serves. Like her, they pour their lives into the work. Amy moves to phase three of expansion – engagement of indigenous peoples.

***

With Grant's interest, I keep going. "I find it interesting because it still applies to today."

"How's that?"

"I find a lot of people are tired of church-going today. Think of all the leaders in arts and industry sitting in the pew. They might enjoy listening to a sermon on Sunday morning, but I don't think they enjoy just sitting. They have leadership skills. They use them every day. I think they want to help out. Sometimes there is little for them to do. They don't want to sit on committees. They already have enough meetings."

Grant agrees, "Good point."

"Why isn't there a place for them to lead? They want to use the same talents and gifts in the church that they use every day, otherwise they get bored. Some leave and don't come back. Golf and football are pretty attractive alternatives. On the other hand, when clergy learn how to activate their members, church can be meaningful."

"Yeah. I get what you're saying. It's the same with business. If you don't give people a chance to improve and get ahead in their job – they get bored and move on."

I ask, "Are you retired?"

"Yes. Twice. After the big crash, my retirement crashed too. I had to go back to work."

"What kind of work did you do?"

"I was a foreman for a construction firm. We built houses in Calgary."

"I'm from there too. Let me ask, when you had an employee that did a good job, showed some smarts, did you promote him – maybe make him a foreman?"

"Exactly. It's the only way to keep people."

"Well that's what I'm talking about with the church. I say we need to figure ways to promote and enlist the incredible people who go to church each Sunday. If we don't, we'll lose them. If people get a chance to share in

the direction of the they become committed.
They have a heart for the work. If it's just a matter
of listening to sermons and taking catechism classes,
real leaders get bored."

"Yeah. That reminds me of another friend. When his
workers grow beyond his company, he actually helps
them start their own business. He isn't afraid of the
competition. He isn't scared they'll take his work away."

I try to connect the two parts of the conversation – his
work and my book; "Do you ever go to church?"

"I used to. I don't go any more. I was brought up in a
strict reformed church."

I've spent years in the Lutheran and Reformed wing of
the church. When he says 'strict' I know what he means.

He continues, "I stopped going. I felt judged all
the time. I didn't agree with some of the teachings and
there wasn't a lot of room for that. Now I keep it simple.
I believe the important thing is to do good to others.
Don't harm anyone. You know, don't lie. Don't cheat
anyone – those kinds of things. I just try to live a
good life."

Grant seems sincere. There's a lot of history behind
his remark.

I risk a question. "How's that going for you?" I ask.
"Do you think you're able to live a good life?"

"I try."

"Can I ask you something? I am curious for my own
sake. What do you do about guilt? What about all the
faults and failings that are part of everyday life? How do
you deal with that?"

Grant shrugs, "We all have guilt, don't we?"

"For sure – but doesn't guilt make it hard to be good? I find guilt kills the motivation. When I try to be good, guilt handcuffs me."

Grant nods. "I can see that."

Grant seems open, so I press on.

"I just wonder what you think. You've been to church. You know the story. I have a question. If all God wants from us is to live a good life, then why is Jesus on the cross? Why didn't he just come and show us how to live a good life?"

"That's a good question. I'm not sure."

"Isn't one reason, because we need to get rid of guilt before we can start to be good? My understanding is that Jesus came to die so he could forgive us and remove the barrier of guilt. That's what paves the way to living a good life."

He thinks for a few seconds. He says, "That makes sense."

"I find guilt doesn't just go away. Psychologists like Freud agree. Guilt hangs around making life miserable. I can try to ignore guilt but guilt won't ignore me."

Grant is quiet but listening.

"I think guilt is like toxic waste – PCBs- something that is deadly but takes millions of years to get rid of. I heard of some people who tried to bury PCBs a mile underground. A few years later it surfaced. It had seeped through fissures in the rocks."

"I think I heard something about that."

"Sure we have to be good. But good isn't the biggest challenge. We also have to figure out what to do about our wrongs and sins. You know, what's in the heart."

Grant hesitates, "Hmmm."

I'm not sure Grant is comfortable with where the discussion is headed.

My cigar is winding down. So is our conversation. Before it goes up in smoke I need to listen to what Grant thinks. I can tell he has some things he wants to say.

Just then Grant's wife comes by. She's heading to the pool. He says he will join her in a few minutes.

He picks up the discussion. He lets me know the heart of his concerns. "I have a problem with some Christians- the ones who talk about hell. I can't believe that everyone who is not a Christian is just going to hell. My mom used to say, 'Every Jew and every Catholic is going to hell. No exceptions.'"

"That's a lot of people who don't have a chance. No wonder you were upset."

"Yeah. I dated a Jewish girl once. My mother was so disappointed. I could tell. She just scowled when I told her."

"I guess you met some bigotry."

"Yes I did. But my mom eventually softened up years later. She wasn't nearly so strict in her old age."

Changing his expression from 'my mother' to 'my mom' says a lot. I can tell she was a big part of his life- and his journey. Her words used to hurt. Maybe later her words healed.

Grant butts out his cigarette and keeps talking. He returns to his burden with strict religion.

"Yeah, there is a lot of bigotry and fighting started by that kind of religion. Just think of the Catholics and Protestants in Ireland. Killing each other because of their beliefs."

I should probably just listen. Instead I comment, "I like to think they kill each other in spite of their beliefs."

"What do you mean?"

"People kill people. Think of Hitler or Stalin. They killed a lot of people too. Millions in fact. They didn't believe in religion."

"Yeah, that's true."

"I think when people decide to kill people, they just use religion as an excuse. Think of the recent beheadings done in the name of Islam. These are people filled with hate and anger. They use religion to justify their killings."

"I see what you mean."

"There is a reason church people get it wrong. They forget what Jesus is all about. Instead of letting God do the judging, they start judging. I think Christianity is pretty simple. It's about following Jesus. All our beliefs and practices don't mean much if we don't end up following and getting to know him."

Grant looks at me. Maybe he agrees. I'm not sure. He goes back to his Jewish girlfriend.

"Things didn't work out with me and my Jewish girlfriend but I'm glad my mom had a change of heart. Later she admitted she was wrong. She realized I had to choose my own beliefs."

My cigar is down to a last puff. Our conversation is too. I don't feel bad that I had to stop reading my book. Grant seems glad to have talked. There has been a friendly openness throughout our conversation.

I offer a final thought. I have a reason.

"There is something else just as important as getting rid of guilt- another thing we can't solve ourselves. Do you know what that is?"

"I'm not sure."

"Each of us is going to die. Even if we imagine we can be good not one of us can beat death."

I'm looking at someone seriously overweight, and a heavy smoker.

"You're right about that."

"You and I are going to die. For each of us the clock is ticking. At our age, it is closer than it was."

Grant nods, "You're right."

"Do you believe in an afterlife"?

"Yes I still do. I believe in God. In fact, I believe in heaven and hell."

I'm surprised. A lot of people who stop going to church still believe in an afterlife. Not many believe in a final day of reckoning. Grant has given up on church but not on the hope of a life after this one.

I explain my question, "In the Bible we find two things about Jesus. For one he died to remove our guilt but, second, he raises from the dead to give us everlasting life."

"I understand."

I tell him my story – about finding God.

"When I was 17 someone read a Bible passage to me. They read it out loud and slowly. It was about the end of the world. It was from Matthew 24. I was convicted. I thought to myself, 'John you are going to hell.' I had lived a pretty crazy and selfish life up to that point. The thought of final judgment scared me.'

"Then it occurred to me – if there's a hell then there's also a heaven."

Grant seems dialed in. "So what happened?"

"Basically I did the math. I can live forever and ever if I trust myself to Jesus. Or I can suffer judgment for my sins."

"It was easy to choose. I trusted Jesus and asked God for eternal life. He answered me. He took away my guilt in an instant and filled my heart with his Spirit. I found hope, real hope, for the first time ever. I still have it."

Now Grant is the one who is surprised. He sits upright. His eyes are fixed on mine. I can tell he is impacted.

Glancing at my watch, I notice less than thirty minutes have passed. The conversation has moved from polite to interesting to intense. We've covered a lot of ground.

We get up and say our goodbyes. As we shake hands, I wonder something. I wonder, "Could I be the answer to a mother's prayer?"

This is the reason why I decided to press on and be bold. I imagine a mom who finally learned to love her son the way she always wanted to. I also imagine a mom who wanted her son to find his way back to God.

As for Grant, I hope I helped him. I'm sure our conversation was meant to be. When we met, his faith is up in smoke, but I am pretty sure there are embers. Where there are embers there is always hope for a flame. I like to think we stirred up some embers during our smoke time. I hope our conversation rekindled his search for God.

Freedom or Fundamentalism

It starts out with a scrap. It ends with an epiphany.

I head out to play golf with a friend. We guys are competitive when it comes to our games. Forbes estimates a total annual revenue (2014) for all sports to be over $450 billion. Suffice it to say, sports is not a matter of indifference.

Golf is an individual sport, but it can get ugly if someone gets wrapped up in playing their best game ever. They can get downright sullen. With Wilson and I matches are a friendly competition. I know he is going to win every time. Still I try.

This applies to discussions about religion. They might get a bit competitive, but they can remain friendly.

People say the possibility of a quarrel is a good r eason to avoid politics and religion. I don't agree. I find the best way to grow in my own faith is to open it up to a challenge.

We only argue about what matters to us. Religion is the domain of our deepest hopes and fears about what is true and real. Truth, forgiveness and salvation are in the religion department. We feel strongly about these things. We should. In present times many are willing to die for their beliefs – hundreds and thousands, all over the world.

The course we play is spectacular. I narrowly lose – only by eight strokes. On the drive back, the conversation turns from golf to religion. I bring up the recent terrorist attacks in Northern Syria. Fundamentalism has turned to beheadings, kidnappings, and trafficking. School girls, rural peasants, and university students are the new martyrs.

I say, "It is incredible to think it, but people imagine God to be on their side. They are willing to kill to prove it."

I'm not trying to be controversial. I don't even intend to get into a God conversation. I don't anticipate my comment will provoke a strong reaction. I'm wrong.

I hit a nerve. The conversation takes a big hook. Wilson fires away. "All religions breed fanatics like this. This is the basic problem in the world. Christian fundamentalism, Islamic fundamentalism – it's fundamentalism that is the problem."

My response is knee jerk. "I can't believe you'd say that. You mean to tell me that the teachings of Jesus are no different than the teachings of jihad? You couldn't be more wrong."

So far, not a good start to a friendly discussion.

Wilson seems unfazed.

He counters, "Religion has a way of begetting bigots."

"Besides, what do we really know about what Jesus really said? The Bible has been written and rewritten so many times over the centuries, no one has a clue."

I know a little about this. "Are you sure about that?"

"Oh yeah. The guys in power kept the teachings that fit their agenda and edit everything else. It's all about power."

These are strong accusations. Now I face two hazards. On one hand, Christianity produces fundamentalists. On the other, the Bible is propaganda.

I know a hasty temper makes for a lousy God conversation. I try to stay calm. Still, I'm not just going to lay-up on this one.

****

We are at the edge of a scrap. I'm feisty when challenged – a definite weakness when it comes to fruitful dialogue. I grew up in an immigrant family with two older brothers. We liked to fight.

We round a turn in the road. I can't help noticing, it's a beautiful day. The orchards are ripe for picking. Trees are collapsing with yellow pears and red apples. It's a good day in the Okanagan Valley.

I try to be reasonable. "Wilson, you've been listening to propaganda. I've done a good deal of study on the reliability of Biblical documents. Did you know that many of the best scholars are confident the New Testament was completed by 90 AD? Even those unsympathetic with the Bible say that the text we have is pretty much what was written by the original writers."

Wilson doesn't answer. Maybe he is thinking it over. Maybe he doesn't have a reply. Most people don't know who wrote the Bible. There's a lot of careless information when it comes to the Bible. There are deep sand traps of ignorance and apathy.

At this point I think I'm more interested in winning the argument than listening to Wilson. I say to myself, "Just drop it. Leave it lie."

Wilson isn't in the mood to stop. He takes a different line. "Look. What the Bible says is a matter of interpretation. Christians argue among themselves about what is true. Every group interprets the Bible in the way that suits them. Since day one Christians have been divided. Look at all the different Christian denominations and religions."

He adds, "If Christianity is true, why can't Christians agree and get along? All the different religions from the same Bible just proves my point."

I stop to think about what Wilson is saying. I grant Christians disagree a lot. This is a black eye for Jesus' followers. There are bunches of denominations and major rifts among the billion or so Christians. Sects and cults abound. There are lots of fundamentalists that are no fun to be around.

I could try to argue how certain basic truths unite all Christians. Most people who own the name 'Christian' affirm the same Apostle's Creed. All denominations since the earliest of times affirm that God created the world from nothing – by his word. Christ is God. He was born by miracle, lived by miracles, died to remove sin, and was raised to life by miracle. The Bible is God's word. There will be a day of reckoning. Each of us has a 'little black box' called a conscience. It records our thoughts words and deeds. One day it will be 'play back time' for everyone. God will judge the world. There is forgiveness and eternal life for all who believe in Christ.

Still, I have to grant there are a lot of denominations and fractures.

Instead I hold back. I feel a nagging thought rising to consciousness. I want to follow that feeling. I ask myself, "What doesn't fit here? Why are my 'spidey senses' tingling?"

Suddenly I'm hit with a realization. A new thought dawns. You might say I have an epiphany. The word 'epiphany' literally means 'surrounded by light.' Anytime you're broadsided by an important truth, it has this epiphany effect. God gives epiphanies.

I no longer care about winning the argument. Wilson's challenge brings me to an important insight – something essential about my own faith.

I'm willing to concede the point about divided Christians. I leave this behind. I change directions and start asking Wilson a few questions.

"So Wilson, can I ask, do you value the right to hold your own opinions and beliefs?"

"Absolutely."

"Is it okay for you and me and anyone else to hold differing views – even if their views are unpopular?"

"Sure."

"And do you believe that you should have the right to voice your views freely and strongly, even if half the world disagrees with you?"

No need to think this over. "For sure," he says.

I agree as well.

"You realize, don't you, that there are lots of places in the world where people are not free to voice their convictions. Coercion and punishment are used to ensure compliance to a given set of convictions and beliefs."

"Okay?" I can tell he is wondering where these questions are leading.

"In fact there are times and places, even today, where it would be dangerous to argue the views you hold. You wouldn't be free to challenge a religious person with your views. There are places where speaking against religion could be a felony, maybe a capital offense."

"Yes, that's true. That's how crazy fundamentalism is."

"Aren't you glad to live in a place where you can argue your view out loud, freely, publicly, with no fear of being silenced or censored?"

"Yeah... We live in the best place in the world. What's your point?"

"Okay, I'll tell you. Let's go back to the thing about Christians disagreeing. You say they hold all kinds of different views, even arguing their beliefs strongly."

"That's what I said."

"So Christians have a lot of different opinions about their beliefs. At the same time they feel free to state with passion what they believe to be true."

"Yeah. And...?"

"Well we just agreed that the freedom to hold different views and to express them freely is a good thing, right?"

No reply.

"Well, isn't the freedom to disagree a good thing for Christians too? Isn't it a wonderful reality about an open society that atheists and religious people are free to hold to and argue different views?"

"Hmm."

"You don't want people to have to believe the same things. Nor do I. In fact we insist it shouldn't be so."

I share my epiphany. "So why should Christians all believe the same things? In fact isn't it essential that Christians be allowed to hold and argue different views – just like everyone else? Finding the truth requires the freedom to hold and to argue our different beliefs."

"The fact that Christians are divided because of different views isn't a weakness. It's a strength. When Christians allow freedom of expression, it proves they are on a quest for truth. It proves they respect the right of others to have the same quest. In fact, the free public discourse you and I enjoy is one of the great freedoms rising out of a Christian society. Since the reformation in the 16th century, Christians have fought for freedom of religion and freedom of speech – they go hand in hand. That's why both are central in our Charter of Rights."

***

We head over the last rise. The lake is shimmering with the light of day. When it comes to golf, Wilson beats me soundly. He's better than I am. I don't mind him winning. I enjoy playing. There will be a next time.

Our little disagreement turns into an epiphany. I have learned some important and precious things about my own faith. After a rocky start, this ends up being a good God conversation. I hope there will be others.

PART 3:
GOING DEEP:
Inviting God into
the Conversation

When You Haven't Got a Prayer

I am in town for a few days to visit my mother and other family members. My mother informs me, "Karl is in a bad way. His cancer is winning and he probably doesn't have long to live." Karl was a good friend of my father, before dad passed away. Mom suggests, "Why don't you drop by and visit him?"

Next morning I go by the hospital. I walk into the room. Family surrounds Karl. They would like to have words. They want to be strong. They just don't know what to say. "Hi John," they greet me politely, but with little enthusiasm. Karl's four grown sons look down, awkward in the situation. These boys are used to being strong but now they are cowed. No one is in charge when death is in the room.

Karl's wife doesn't know what to say either. She whispers, "Please don't upset him."

I turn to look at Karl. He is curled up on the bed.

His head is swollen twice its normal size. He appears comatose and is heavily sedated. Karl is in the last stages of brain cancer. I don't think his family has ever been in a room with a dying person before – much less their father.

I'm a friend of the family so they're open to my visit. Still, I am pretty sure they don't want me to talk about God, death, and the afterlife. At the same time, studies show that many of those near death want the truth out in the open. Prayer and discussions about God are usually welcome – if the one sharing is gentle and has some wisdom.

I turn to Karl's wife and say, "Okay. But you don't mind me praying for him do you?" She nods, "That would be okay."

I edge over to the side of the bed and sit on a chair. I face Karl, opposite his swollen face. His eyes are closed. I'm not sure he can hear me.

I take his hand. I begin to pray a simple prayer. I speak slowly and deliberately. It goes something like this...

"Father, I don't know if Karl can hear me, but I know you can speak to him. You know Karl. I pray that he would know peace at this time and that you would give him courage in this battle. You forgive us for asking. We do ask for your kind mercy. You are the good shepherd. You guide us through the darkest valley. Teach us to trust in your might and care. We do not need to fear when you are with us. I pray you would give Karl strength in both body and soul. Give him faith and courage to trust you at this time – to know your strength and hope."

In the middle of my prayer I notice something.

It's Karl. He's definitely squeezing my hand. His eyes are closed. He can't speak but he is responding the only way he can – through touch.

I am stirred by this. I'm sure Karl wants me to continue.

"Father, you know each of us intimately and personally. You made us for yourself and our hearts find rest only in you. You are quick to forgive and hear our prayers. Please hear Karl's inner prayer in his very difficult and dark time. Help him to give you all his sorrow and pain. Hold him in your hand. Though we walk through the shadow of death you are with us. Outwardly we are wasting away, but inwardly we are being renewed. I pray that by your amazing grace in Christ that you will renew his inner being. Give him hope and faith, and comfort in his suffering."

Karl's grip doesn't lessen. If anything it grows stronger. His pressure is firm and his hand is warm. I open my eyes for a minute. I see a tear coming down Karl's bloated face. This is heart warming and heart rending...beautiful.

Karl is not given to crying. A burly man, for years he has been a no nonsense construction manager – not sentimental in the least. Still, right now, listening to my prayer, Karl is weeping.

I take heart. I glance up for a brief second. The family look okay. I continue, only now my prayer goes deeper. "Father, I thank you that nothing can separate us from your love. It doesn't matter what the obstacle or pain is, you can carry us through. You give hope and eternal life to anyone who trusts in you. You forgive all our failings when we ask you to. You are the resurrection and the life. There is no sickness that is stronger than you.

You heal both body and soul. Please help us to believe in you – and to trust you in this dark and difficult time. Strengthen Karl, I pray. Give him faith. Help him to trust you. Give him courage and hope that can never be taken away. I ask for these things in the name of your only son, who willingly gave himself us – and gives forgiveness and eternal life to all who ask. I pray this for Karl. Amen."

Karl is still holding my hand as I finish this prayer. When I say, "Amen" he gives my hand a firm squeeze before letting go. His eyes are still wet.

I sit still for a minute. No one says anything. No one has too. It has been transcendent to say the least. I think we all feel something or Someone in the room.

Eventually I stand up. I say my goodbyes. As I walk down the hospital corridor, I feel warm with gratitude. I am immersed in thankfulness. My time of prayer with Karl has not been an accident. God meant it to be. God had something to say to a child he loves. He sent me to pray with him. It is God's way and I am glad.

I know when I pray for Karl I invite God into the conversation. When I pray, I become part of God's conversation with Karl.

I tell myself, "I hope to meet Karl in heaven one day."

He dies a few days later.

She Learns to Have Conversations with God through Hell and High Water

Since she was a little girl, Susan has prayed every day. No one has taught her how. She prays for her friends, loved ones, and people in need – pretty much the whole world. She attends church occasionally – more in recent years.

I know Sue well. We're good friends. She's also my sister.

During a difficult, no, a horrendous year of her life, she invites me to teach her how to pray.

When our training starts, Sue is battling breast cancer. She has her meltdowns but she's a fighter who doesn't know the word 'quit.' A vast team of friends and family rally around her. They raise a ton of money for cancer research. Sue has the ability to rally people to a good cause. Even with a full time job she finds time to volunteer for the national director position of Ronald MacDonald House.

I pray with her over the phone. I ask God to heal her body and to strengthen her soul. She loves that.

***

One day at the family summer cottage we get talking.
I ask her, "Would you like to learn more about prayer?
I'd be happy to come alongside and help." Some years
earlier she read a book called "Seven Days of Prayer
with Jesus." It's about Jesus' prayer. She found it
encouraging.

"I would love that, John."

We sit beside each other in a well-lit corner.
The sunlight streams across the deck. We face a
sylvan lake. It's a beautiful summer day.

We talk about the suffering and pain and get talking
about prayer. I ask her, "Why does Jesus encourage us
to call God 'Our Father'?"

"Well God loves us and takes care of us, right?"

"Did you know that God has more than a hundred
names in the Bible, but Jesus uses only one. He calls
God 'Father' every time. The one exception – on the
cross he cries 'My God my God why have you forsaken
me?' Why do you think that is?"

"Well God must want us to think of him in a very
personal way."

"Right. God is not just an 'anybody' God. He's a
personal God. He's our Father because he created us.
He becomes our Father, in the deepest sense, as we
trust him for everything in life."

Sue nods, "Okay. I get that."

I expand, "Anyone can call him God, and pray to him,
but those who become his children by faith get to call
him 'Father.' The word Jesus uses to pray is 'Abba.'
It means 'Daddy.'

"Wow. That's so beautiful." Sue is very expressive.

"Jesus became a man so that we could become children of God. We have the same child-and-father status Jesus enjoys with God. One verse in the Bible says, 'Behold what manner of love the Father has given unto us, that we should be called children of God.' Someone else said the same thing another way, 'The Son of God became the Son of Man, so that the Sons of Men could become Sons of God.'"

Sue's eyes are shining. "That's so amazing. I'm so glad I can call God 'Father'."

After I leave, we continue to pray together over the phone. It's a few months later before we continue our conversation face to face. In the meantime, Sue is in the middle of her fight with cancer. She has had a mastectomy and is enduring chemo and radiation treatment. She has lost her hair.

We spend time catching up. I try to listen and engage my heart. I want to feel something of what she is going through. The topic turns to prayer. I ask Sue how her prayer life is going.

"Really good. I always call God 'Father' when I pray. It makes me feel close to God."

"Do you want to hear another cool thing you can pray?"

"Absolutely."

The second big thing about prayer is that when you pray to God the Father you need to pray in Jesus' name." "Okay. Really? Tell me why."

I explain, "It has to do with God's nature. God is entirely love, but at the same time he is completely holy. He is absolutely perfect in everything he is, everything he says, and everything he does. God is holy in his love and he is loving in his holiness."

Sue takes a few seconds to think this over. "Yeah. I can see that. He has to be that way. Okay, how does that fit in with praying in Jesus' name?"

"Well it does, in a very important way. For one, you and I can't just wander into God's presence with our sins and failings. The Bible tells us, 'O Lord, your eyes are too holy to look upon evil.' We need forgiveness and healing and cleansing in order to be in the presence of God. We need to be holy in order to stand before a holy God."

"Are you saying we can't just pray and expect God to answer?"

"Right. But this is the good news, the very best news. This is what the good news of the gospel is all about. This is why Jesus came to earth. This is why he was willing to die."

Sue's eyes are wide open. So is her heart.

"When Jesus dies an amazing miracle happens. There is a great exchange. When he dies on the cross – he takes the sin of the world on his shoulders. When he dies he imparts his perfect righteousness to those who believe in him."

"How does that work?"

"Right. When we say, 'In Jesus' name' at the end of a prayer – we acknowledge it is only because of him that we can pray at all. Because of him we can call God Father. Because of him God accepts us as his holy children. This is the whole reason prayer is a 24/7 reality."

"Do I ever need that. I'm going to start praying in Jesus' name."

"It's not just a phrase. These words transform our prayer time completely. He carried our sins and sorrows on the cross and he carries us into the presence of God. Now we get to stay there forever. Like sons and daughters we have continual, uninterrupted intimate audience with God. I often picture myself like a little child, jumping up on his knee and just letting him hug me."

***

A few months later, Sue has come a long way. Her cancer is in remission. Her hair is growing back. Considering the tough time she has been through – Sue is doing great.

She also finds a vibrant church and meets new friends that embrace her. Sue gets to know the pastor and his wife and goes to their home group. She tells me, "I just love going to church. It brings meaning and joy into my life." Her daughter Taylor gets lots out of it too. Her husband tries for a while, but is not really interested. Still, it seems the tide has turned for the good.

Then it happens. Another bomb drops. After 17 years together, after sharing this terrible battle with cancer, her husband tells her he wants to leave the marriage. Sue is leveled.

They try counseling. It doesn't take root. After months of anguish and empty hopes, Sue realizes it's over.

Over the phone we talk and pray together. The confusion, the anger, the tears come pouring out. She tells me this breakup is harder than fighting cancer. She is deeply shaken. Still, she takes her hurts to God and shares them openly with those who love her. They come alongside. Her friends at church pray with her. We continue our brother-sister relationship over the phone. I try to help. I've never felt more of a brother than now.

***

One day she asks the obvious question. "John, maybe you can help me. How come I get to know God, I start to follow him, and then everything falls apart? I just don't get it."

As I listen I try to understand. Hurt doesn't describe what she is going through.

I want to help, "Susan, I wonder if there might be a different way to look at it." She looks at me with questions in her eyes.

"I know you've had a lot of hard things happen Sue. You have a lot of tears, but you have a lot of courage too."

"I don't feel very courageous."

"I know. But let me ask, don't you think God knew ahead of time what you would be going through? Doesn't it make sense that He met you, made you his special child, so that he could carry you through all these troubles?"

"I want to believe that."

"He's a big God. Nothing is beyond his care for you. None of this has taken him by surprise."

"Yeah. That has to be right."

"I'm sure that's what's going on. Far from abandoning you to the trials, God has come to you at just the right time – just when he knows you most need him. He loves you so much he has come into your heart and life when you can't possibly face these troubles without him."
"That makes sense. It still hurts, but it helps."

***

Summer comes round again. It's been another long year for Sue. It's also a year or so since we started our prayer talks. It's another sunny day at the cottage. We're sitting in the same corner as before. After catching up, we get around to a third prayer lesson.

"How is your prayer life coming along Sue?"
"Really great, John. Every time I pray I call God Father. I end my prayers saying 'in Jesus' name.'"

"Terrific. How does that make you feel?"

She thinks for a minute. "You know what? I enjoy praying more and more. When I'm filled with anxiety, I pray to God and he gives me peace. I know I can talk to my father about anything. I know that because Jesus died for me, I can come to God any time and he hears my prayers."

"Sue, you're growing by leaps and bounds. You can't believe how much you're encouraging me."

She beams.

"I know about a third important lesson of prayer? Are you interested?"

"Of course I am. Go for it."

"Here it is. Every day I always ask God to fill me with his Holy Spirit."

"Okay. What does that mean? I didn't know I should do that."

"We need at least three things from God in order to live life with joy and hope. First we need to know God as our Father. Second, we need forgiveness through Jesus. We talked about that. One more thing – the third thing – we also need healing and the power to live life like sons and daughters of God. None of us has the strength and power to live this life on our own."

"Okay. So this is important. How do we get that?"

"Power for life is all about asking each day for the Holy Spirit to fill us. The Spirit brings us into the healing joy and power of Christ."

I use an illustration, "In the book of Revelation chapter 22, you can read about a great river that flows from God's throne and from the presence of Christ." Sue asks, "What does the river do?"

"Well, like any river, it brings water for replenishing. There are trees on either side of the river. They bear fruit every month of the year. This river provides drinking water. It provides water for cleansing. Those who immerse in this water find healing and new life. This river is a picture of the Holy Spirit. When Jesus ascended to heaven he poured out his Holy Spirit like a river into the hearts of every believer. Like a great and deep stream, the Holy Spirit brings healing and refreshment to our souls. The Holy Spirit is the source of all of our power for living."

Sue takes a minute to respond. "I never thought of it that way. So is that why we get the Holy Spirit when we believe?"

"Right. Jesus says, 'I stand at the door and knock, if anyone hears and opens, my father and I will come in and make our home with him.' Not only do we get to be in God's presence but God will come to live right in our hearts. The very minute someone trusts in Christ and opens the door, the Holy Spirit comes to live within them. Every true believer has the Spirit of Christ, the Holy Spirit living within."

"Okay, but tell me something. If we have the Holy Spirit within us, why do we have to ask for more each day?"

"Good question. It's about replenishing. We are given the Holy Spirit when we believe, but we are also invited to be filled with the Holy Spirit. Jesus encourages us to pray for the Holy Spirit before anything else. Filling is a matter of degree. We can be more or less filled. God won't leave us but the tank can run dry. Jesus promises, 'Much more will your heavenly father give the Holy Spirit to those who ask.' Another passage says, 'always be filled with the Holy Spirit.' Jesus wants us to ask for the Holy Spirit every day and he promises to fill us each time."

"Okay. I think I get it. I understand. If I want everything God has to give me I have to pray three things. I need to call God 'Father.' I pray 'in Jesus name." Third, I am going to ask God to fill me with his Spirit. "

I smile. She smiles. "Amen!"

Sue is still praying these three things.

Outwardly Wasting, Inwardly Renewing

It's near the end. I hold Ted's hand and pray with him. I recite verses from the Psalms and the words of Jesus. He is silent, forcing a smile with his eyes. Only his eyes have any light left. Everything else is dark. Emaciated from cancer, Ted is resigned to the outcome. When I first met him, he was about 5'8" and 180 pounds. Now, three years later, Ted is less than 100 pounds. Outwardly he has wasted away, inwardly he is renewed, at the threshold of a new life.

With affectionate memories, I look back on the several conversations of our three-year friendship.

***

I meet Ted in November 2008 after we move into our summer cottage in Okanagan Center. He runs the corner store. I retreat to the cottage a few days every month or so – mostly during the winter. My life is busy and a regular time alone is something to which I really look forward. Every few days I walk over to the store to get basics.

I notice Ted doesn't look healthy. He is only in his mid-fifties, but his skin is ashen-grey. He is shy but friendly. We always exchange small talk.

Ted lives alone. He doesn't get much business in the winter. Most people just drop by to pick up milk or eggs and say hi. One day I stop by. Ted is sitting in front of a TV screen. The light is low. He is watching a hockey game.

He looks a little rumpled and sad. I think this is normal for Ted. Old hurts are written on his eyes and never really go away, until the last few weeks of his life.

I ask "Hey Ted, would you like some company. I like to watch hockey."

"Sure" he says.

This becomes our habit for the next two winters. We both enjoy hockey. We banter about who deserves to win or lose, who will score the most goals, and how we're frustrated when our favorite team can't seem to get traction.

***

Some eighteen months before the end, I come by the store. There are no customers. Ted looks down-hearted, even more than usual. His eyes are heavy and dark. I ask if everything is okay.

"I just found out I have cancer. It looks pretty bad." Ted says this in a matter of fact way, but I hear the fear. I feel the aloneness.

"Oh no. Tell me it's not true, Ted. I'm so sorry."

"I go in next week to find out about treatment."

"That's hard."

"Yeah."

"Do you want to talk about it?"

"No. I don't think so, but thanks."

"Well I'll be praying for you. You can count on that."
This might be a first for Ted. He looks quizzical, and
appreciative at the same time. After a pause, he says,
"I would like that."

Feeling the weight of the moment. I take a small risk.
"I don't want to be seem presumptuous Ted, but would
you mind if I say a brief prayer for you now?"

Pause. "Well, okay... sure."

I pray a simple prayer, something like this: "Father,
I pray for Ted. I'm sorry to hear of his cancer. I know
it is hard. I pray that you'll be with Ted to help him
through this. Give him courage. Grant him healing.
We will thank you for your help. I pray in Jesus' name."

"Thanks John. I appreciate that."

This becomes the first of many times I pray with Ted.

***

Some weeks later, I drop by and Ted is watching
hockey again. He likes Toronto. I like Calgary. His team
is playing. He is happy for me to sit and join him.

I know Ted is wrestling with life and death. Like all of
us, when he wakes in the middle of the night, he has to
face the demons alone.

As we get talking, Ted lets me into his past.
He tells me that he is estranged from his family and
seldom sees his children. This is the 'other hurt' in his
life. As a wise king Solomon put it, "The heart knows its
own bitterness."

Ted is a private person. He changes topics. "I started
treatments this week. I'll be doing this for the next
three or four months, and then they'll decide if I need
radiation."

"That has to be pretty scary."
He looks at me, "Yeah. Well. I guess... Yeah it is."

Ted explains the regimen to me. After treatments, they send him home with pills that are part of his treatment. I know he will be given painkillers at some point. At first he doesn't want them.

I offer to pray for him again.

This time his response is less cautious. "I'd like that."

This time I pray a little longer. I go a little deeper. I put my hand on his shoulder.

I pray something like this: "Father, I bring Ted before you. He is facing some deep sorrows and tough trials. I pray you would give him courage and help him conquer his fears. I pray you will do the same for me – when I am overcome by my fears. I recall the psalm that says, 'I cried out to the Lord and he delivered me from all my fears.' Help us as we cry out to you."

I pause for a minute before continuing, "I pray that you will grant healing and courage to Ted – healing to his body and courage for his soul. Give the doctors wisdom and bless the treatments. We know that You are our healer, and that You can do all things. I pray especially you will help Ted to give his cares and his fears to you.' I pause for a minute to give Ted a chance to silently pray if he feels like it. I end, "And because Jesus knows all about our sorrow and pain, I ask this in Jesus' name."

I hear a heavy sigh. I feel his shoulders rise and fall. A prayer goes deeper than any other words. Prayer brings God into the conversation.

***

A few months later I visit the store. Ted's weight loss is visible. His face is thinner. A belt is drawn tight over sagging pants that are now way too big. We have a good visit. I ask about his family, whether they know how he is doing and when they might visit. He tells me about a divorce that went sour and about kids and grandkids he used to see all the time. He doesn't show a lot of emotion but I know this is the central hurt of his life. Even the cancer doesn't go as deep. Maybe this explains his silent retreat from the world.

I offer to pray. This time, Ted has been waiting for me to offer. His body is hurting and his spirit is heavy. I put my hand on his shoulder. We both bow our heads. I pray a longer prayer, and add some of the Bible passages I am familiar with, especially the Psalm 23. This psalm of David is a light in dark times for those who suffer.

"The Lord is my Shepherd, I shall not want.
He makes me to lie down in green pastures.
He leads me beside the still waters. He restores my soul.
He leads me in paths of righteousness for his names sake
Yea though I walk through the valley of the shadow of death I will fear no evil.
You are with me. Your rod and your staff comfort me."

***

The next time we have an extended visit is a few months later. It's late spring. Flowers are beginning to open and trees are budding. Everything is coming to life. The lake shimmers with light. Inside the store is a different matter. There's no hint of spring. The light is dim. Ted is worse for wear. He's lost about 25 pounds. This is an aggressive cancer, maybe stage 4. I don't ask.

Ted's decay has spread to the store. Entering, a person can feel his exhaustion. It sits heavy on the place. Ted used to keep everything ship-shape. Now the shelves are barely stocked. DVDs are scattered on the counter behind the cash register. The fridges have a build up of ice. His desk is a mess – littered with bills and records.

Ted is sitting on his favorite chair. I sit next to him. We don't chitchat so much any more. After greetings and touching base, I ask Ted about his experience with God and religion.

"I used to pray. I don't much anymore."

"Tell me about it."

He seems reluctant but willing at the same time. I think he knows he needs to discuss his past. "My wife became a Jehovah's Witness. This is how we brought up our family. I used to read the books, say the prayers and practice the religion."

"Really? What happened?"

"Well my wife and I grew apart and we got divorced. That was the same time I stopped my involvement with the Witnesses and pretty much stopped praying."

Ted didn't seem to want to say anymore about his private life. It's hard for him. He makes a reference to 'strict religion.'

I offer to pray. Ted says "Sure. Please. I would appreciate it."
Before I do, I ask "Ted would you like to pray along with me?"

"I'm not sure."

"How about saying the words after I say them? That might make it easier – just a way to help out."

"Well maybe."
"Let me start and then you can try if you feel like it."

I begin, "Dear Father, thank you for being kind and merciful…"

I wait through an awkward silence. After a generous pause, I assume Ted doesn't want to pray out loud.

I am about to continue, and then I hear him, his voice quiet and halting, "Dear Father, thank you for being kind and merciful..."

I keep the prayer short. I recite a few Bible verses from the gospels. Ted repeats them. I continue, "But thank you for the good news that you are the resurrection and the life." I add a few other short sentences. Ted repeats phrase after phrase.

Then I finish, "And we pray in Jesus' name. Amen." Ted takes his time on this one. A Jehovah's Witness does not pray to Jesus. He waits a second – and then says, "And we pray in Jesus' name. Amen."

Before I go I say, "Hey Ted, I'm glad we could pray together. Thanks for the privilege."

**

The next time we meet, we both pray again. After we pray, I ask, "Ted, do you find it helpful when I quote Bible verses when we pray?"

"Yes, I do."

"Would you like me to write down some passages that have been a great comfort to me? You can look at them when you feel down or worried. You can recite the passages to God like a prayer."

"Sure. Okay. That might be good."

Before I head back to Vancouver, I write out a dozen or so of my favorite courage and hope passages. I have memorized several for my own times of need:

> *"I cried out to the Lord and he heard me and delivered me from all my fears." (Psalm 34:4)*

> *"Jesus said, 'I am the resurrection and the life. He who believes in me will never die.'" (John 11:17)*

"So we do not lose heart. Though our outer self is wasting away, our inner self is being renewed day by day.". (2 Corinthians 4:16)

I sense his deep need. I feel the fear that crouches, ready to pounce. I start praying for him pretty much each day. I ask others to pray for him too.

***

Time passes. It's now the fall of his last year. The trees have turned brown. The vines are empty. The lake is dark and still. Ted has dwindled to a skeleton. The skin seems to hang on his frame. His eyes are gaunt. He weighs no more than 120 pounds. The disease has taken over. Whatever the chemo is doing, Ted is getting worse. He is going to die, and it won't be long. Ted never complains. Now he's getting radiation treatments and he takes a regular dose of morphine for the pain.

After a few friendly words, I start our times by reading a few passages of Scripture and explain the comfort in them. Then we pray together.

At some point, I bring him a Bible with special passages bookmarked. It is a user-friendly version in today's English. I put a plastic sticky tab in maybe 30 places. I mark several Psalms, key sayings of Jesus, and several passages in the rest of the New Testament that are laced with comfort and hope of eternal life. He says he will read them.

Some passages are just praise and thanksgiving. I explain to Ted that worshipping God is a great way to take his mind off his own troubles and pain. I take time to go through various passages, and explain how he can use the words of God to navigate his pain and trials. We

keep going back to Paul's words in the letter to
the Corinthians: *"Outwardly we are wasting away,
but inwardly we are being renewed day by day."*
(*2 Corinthians 4:16*)

I try to help Ted understand that this world is not all
that there is. A better world waits. Our decaying bodies
will die, but we will live. Every believer will trade in his
old perishing body and get a new one.

I gradually notice a change – not the changes caused
by cancer. I begin to see a light in Ted's eyes. It is a
glimmer of hope.

***

Some weeks later we meet again. Winter has set in.
Ted is down to 100 pounds. He knows he's going to die.
I know he's going to die.

We still pray for his healing but now I want to help
him get ready to die.

"Ted you do not seem to be getting better. Tell me
how things are going."

He is seated behind his old desk, hunched over,
as usual.

He looks up at me. "Not good," he admits.

"You know I hope and pray you will beat this –
but I need to ask. Are you ready to face dying?"
I can see Ted dreads this turn of conversation. I can also
see he is relieved to talk about it.

While he searches for words, I decide to continue,
"I want you to live but I also want to comfort you and
give you courage to face the worst if it happens. Can we
try to do that?"

"Okay. What do you mean?"

"I want you to know that Jesus can take you through anything – even death."

Ted looks at me, inviting me to continue.

"Let me read for you about a powerful event in the life of Jesus. It comes from the gospel of John. Try to put yourself in the picture and to feel the hope."

"There is this man called Lazarus. He dies. Everyone is weeping and mourning in a loud open way – crying and weeping."

I start to read from the gospel of John, chapter 11:

> Lazarus' sister, Martha, says to Jesus, "Rabbi, if you had been here Lazarus would not have died."
>
> Jesus asks her, "Do you believe this?"
>
> Martha says, "Yes. I believe you are the Messiah, sent from God."
>
> Jesus says to her, "Your brother will rise again." Martha said to him, "I know that he will rise again in the resurrection on the last day." Jesus said to her, "I am the resurrection and the life. Whoever believes in me, though he die, yet shall he live, and everyone who lives and believes in me shall never die. Do you believe this?" She said to him, "Yes, Lord; I believe that you are the Christ, the Son of God, who is coming into the world."

At this point Jesus heads over to the cave Lazarus is buried in. He cries out with a loud voice, "Lazarus come out!" Out walks Lazarus , still wrapped in his grave cloths."

I ask Ted, "Are you familiar with the story?"

"I think I read it once."

"Jesus is talking to you and to me here Ted. If you believe in Christ you will be raised from the dead and will live forever with him. Your outer body is wasting

away – but inside you can get stronger every day.
One day you will get a new body that is perfect and
ageless and filled with joy. The life Jesus is talking about
begins today – here and now. What do you think – do
you believe this?

Ted looks up at me. "I want to. I'm not sure."

"How about if we pray? God can help you believe if
you ask him. I am going to pray for you and you can say
the prayer after me if you want."

Ted nods, "Okay."

I pray a prayer one phrase at a time. Ted quietly
whispers each phrase.

"Father, we are suffering here... This body is wasting
away with this cancer... We know you can give new life
even now... and that we can experience the resurrection
Jesus is talking about here... Our faith is weak...
We need help to believe in you... to believe that you can
forgive us of all our sins and give us eternal life... Please
strengthen our faith so we can believe. In Jesus' name
we pray, Amen."

Ted says, "Thanks John. I mean it. This helps."

Through winter and spring I see Ted several more
times. I leave him with a CD of worship songs. He
comes to deeply enjoy them. The choir has some six
different nationalities represented. The music is stirring
and rich.

As the cancer progresses Ted fades away. He takes
oral treatment, radiation, and increased morphine.
I check in on him regularly. I pray with him and ask
if the Bible passages help him. At first he reads the
passages and tells me they are helpful. I notice he still
has a 'New World' translation – the Jehovah's Witness
version, beside him.

As time and cancer progress, Ted stops reading.
He takes a stronger dose of morphine. He says,
"I can't concentrate to read, but I still listen to the
music you gave me. It really gives me strength."

We continue our talks, prayers and Bible reading
each time we meet. I add words from some great
hymns, like "Holy Holy Holy," "Rock of Ages," and
"Great is Thy Faithfulness." Ted is glad for this.
He always says, "Thanks John, for coming by.
It means a lot to me."

***

Summer arrives and we are on family vacation.
As it turns out, our vacation and Ted's passing intersect.
As I look back, I thank God for this. It is no coincidence.

I drop by the store, which is now being run by Ted's
friend. Ted is upstairs.

I climb the steps and walk into his bedroom. There
is a strong smell and I notice alarming stains on the
carpet. Ted has lost bowel control and is now bleeding
internally. I find him curled up – a heap of bones and
skin. He is wasting away, living one breath at a time.

I sit by him. He wakes for a minute. I want to care for
him and comfort him in some way. "Hey Ted. It's rough
isn't it? I know it can't get any harder." He can hardly
whisper. He just nods. I get him water. He sips through
parched cracked lips. I'm deeply moved. I think I am
feeling what God is feeling – I'm sharing the heart of
God for one of his children. Words are helpful but he
also needs touch – like a crying child.

I put my hand on his shoulder. He groans quietly.
I feel his humiliation and pain. I put my hand on his
head and gently stroke it. He quietly lets me. I do this

for a few minutes. I remind him of a few of our favorite passages. I recite one after another from memory.

"Outwardly we are wasting away, but inwardly we are being renewed day by day...God is preparing us for an eternal weight of glory." (2 Corinthians 4:16-17)

"Eye has not seen nor has ear heard nor has the mind of man conceived what God has prepared for those he loves and who are called according to his purpose." (1 Corinthians 2:9)

"Isn't this good news Ted? It won't be long now. Soon there will be peace and rest – a whole new life without any sorrow or disease."

"Yes. Yes."

"You believe this don't you Ted? "Yes." He cringes with pain, "Yes. I do."

I want to comfort him any way I can. I'm not a good singer. Normally I would call my singing painful, but I feel compelled. I sing the words of the "The Lord is my shepherd"... I sing another hymn I have memorized, "Rock of Ages, cleft for me." Ted silently lets it soak in to his weary and broken body. I just sit beside him – until he falls asleep.

***

A few days later I find out Ted's family is visiting. His two daughters have kids. Their visit represents forgetting the past. They want to see their dad and granddad and tell him they love him.

After a few days with Ted, they come over to ask me if I would be willing to plan a memorial for after their dad dies.

"Of course. It would be an honor."

I share a few words of hope with his daughters. I tell them how Ted and I have been getting to know each other. I share how Ted has been getting to know God. I tell them how special it has been to be with Ted and what a privilege it has been to pray with him. They have a good cry.

It turns out there are too many relatives to stay in Ted's home. We have room and private space they can enjoy as a family. As it turns out, they take us up on the offer and stay with us the days before Ted passes and then leading up to the service.

I drop by a few more times in the next week to comfort Ted and pray with him.

***

One morning I find out Ted has gone to hospice care in Kelowna. I go to visit. I find Ted lying in his bed. He is unconscious from all the pain and medication. His two daughters and their children are in the room waiting for the end. They tell me how they had a chance to say goodbye and to hug and cry with their dad.

I sit by Ted. I stroke his head. I quietly say a prayer – filled with comfort and hope from the scriptures. I tell him how thankful I am for our friendship and how glad I am we will meet again in a better world.

After a while I leave the family to be alone with their dad. This is the last time I will see Ted. His life has come full circle. I find out the next day, Ted has passed away.

***

A few days later the whole community gathers to say goodbye to Ted. I know my role. It's my part to help people remember Ted, and maybe let them see a side of him they didn't know.

While people are finding seats, the CD I gave to Ted plays in the background. At the service a daughter and granddaughter share cherished memories of Ted. A neighbor does as well.

When it's my turn, I narrate recent conversations and prayers with Ted. I read some of his favorite passages. I talk about our times of prayer together. From the CD, we play one of the songs, which Ted grew to love. I share how he grew stronger in faith and soul even while his body wasted away.

It is a rich time. There is a warm glow in the room. We all have a chance to remember Ted, and get to know him a little better. There is so much hope. I don't think anyone leaves depressed. There is even a hint of celebration as we all think about Ted's hope for a new life.

Conclusion:
God Is in Conversation
with Every Person

When you talk with someone about God, God is in the conversation. I experience it all the time. God is not just the topic. He is a participant.

My aim in each of these God conversations is to hear God and to help the other person hear him too. I encourage our Sikh taxi driver to make a connection between prayer in the temple and how God is able to inhabit the human heart. I ask Ivan the hitchhiker to consider that God might have a path to us as well as our many paths to God. I challenge the school board leader to go within – and to consider the seven deadly sins with which we all wrestle. I pray with Ted through his terminal cancer so he will find inner renewal from God as his body simply wastes away. As we pray together, we bring God into the conversation.

God wants us to know him. I do not mean that he just wants us to know about him, he wants us to know him in a deep and personal way. He gives us tracks to run on in our quest to find him. He leaves clues to his existence throughout the world and universe. For example, his kindness permeates life and accounts for the abundance of good things we enjoy:

> *"God has not left us without a witness, for he did good by giving you rains from heaven and fruitful seasons, satisfying your hearts with food and gladness."*
> *(Acts 14:17)*

When we stare up at the stars – or we take pictures from the Hubble telescope, we see the might, splendor, and genius of our Maker.

> *The heavens declare the glory of God,*
> *and the sky above proclaims his handiwork.*
> *Day to day pours out speech,*
> *and night to night reveals knowledge.*
> *There is no speech, nor are there words,*
> *whose voice is not heard.*
> *Their voice goes out through all the earth,*
> *and their words to the end of the world. (Psalm 19)*

Quasars, pulsars, star-generating nebula, mind numbing expanses, spiraling galaxies – all remind us of an awesome God.

God is not the creation, but he is present everywhere. In a mysterious way, God pervades every atom and electron. He is in the air we breathe and forms the environment in which we live: *"In him we live and move and have our being."* (Acts 17:28)

God's consciousness fills the world. *"Where can I flee from your presence? Wherever I turn you are there."* (Psalm 139)

The knowledge of God surrounds us and presses in upon us. Even as we 'discover' God, a previous awareness of God comes to the surface.

Let me give a few examples of this, one from family life and one from my conversion.

I recall meeting relatives from Denmark. My parents were immigrants. I was born in Canada so I did not grow up around relatives. Still when I would meet an aunt, uncle or cousin, it was as if I was meeting someone I already knew. Our shared history came to the surface. There was immediate recognition and sense of kinship.

The first time I pray to God I have a similar sense of déjà vu.

I am a troubled teen, wrestling with life. I work for my father's furniture making company. I go to install some cabinets at a convent. During the lunch break I stroll up to the garden. It is lush with flowering bushes. A path winds through it. Every so often, along the path, there is a station with a statue – Mary, Jesus, a cross, or one of the saints. As I walk the pathway I stop here and there to relax. I 'feel' the setting.

A strange thing happens. I sense something familiar. I feel at home somehow. The flower-laden garden is restful. The pathway fits my need to 'find a way.' Everything, even the statues belong in this place. Somehow I belong. It feels like home.

I am invited into this setting. I feel a need to respond. I get down on my knees and pray. "God, I am not sure about you, but I want to know more. I want to believe in you. If you help me find my way, and take this confusion and burden from me, I am yours."

Spiritually and physically, I feel a wave of calm wash over me, from head to toe. My inner knot of angst is removed and peace fills my inmost being.

That day I realize, I am not made for hide and seek. I am made to seek and find.

God is speaking and he wants me to reply. A prayer is how I reply to God.

When I return from work, I tell my girlfriend Caron (now my wife), "I have met an old friend." Indeed I had. I have met God.

When I say that God is in the conversation, I mean he is active and engaged. God is out to get our attention. He is inviting a reply and seeking a dialogue.

In the New Testament we are told that God uses time and geography to encourage people to find him.

> *"He himself gives to all mankind life and breath and everything. And he made from one man every nation of mankind to live on all the face of the earth, having determined allotted periods and the boundaries of their dwelling place, that they should seek God, and perhaps feel their way toward him and find him."* (Acts 17:25 –27)

This is remarkable. We are 'when' we are and 'where' we are so that we can find God. The place and time we live matters when it comes to finding God. I don't presume to understand all his means but there are hints in history. For example, in the first century, a common language, the incredible road grid, and the safety provided by Roman law made it possible for the message of Christ's resurrection to spread throughout the world. In one sense, when it comes to finding God, we are all at the right place at the right time.

An invitation is related to hospitality. This is another way to describe God's conversation with every person. Hospitality is at the heart of Middle Eastern culture. To be invited to dine at someone's home is an honor and privilege. The moment you enter, you are part of the household and given all the privileges of a family member.

Jesus invites us to find him and to 'join the family.' In a vision of his ascended and exalted state, Jesus issues a universal and personal invitation to dine with God. The event is a great wedding banquet.

"Behold, I stand at the door and knock. If anyone hears my voice and opens the door, I will come in to him and eat with him, and he with me." (Revelation 3:20)

A Christian is simply someone who accepts Jesus' generous invitation.

We don't need to come from the Middle East to know that a wedding invitation is significant. It's rude not to respond. If you are family or close friend, it is hurtful.

I once heard of a man who was having difficulties with his family. There was a divorce and everyone separated. Some years later, his daughter was getting married. She came back to where she was brought up to have the wedding. She made sure he got the invitation. Nothing was more important to her than that he attend. She held out the olive branch of reconciliation. Imagine her hurt when he did not reply or attend.

As the father of four daughters I can imagine her hurt. How devastating for a father to neglect the plea of his beloved daughter to come and celebrate her

wedding. If he had come, what healing would result!
What a celebration of life and love. By not coming,
what sorrow and grieving he left behind. I hope there
will (ever) be another chance for this man and his dear
daughter.

We can apply this to God's invitation to us.
He has revealed himself to us every day in presence
and kindness. God made each one of us in his image.
He loves what he has made. He holds out the olive
branch to us – inviting us to celebrate with him.

How much will he be grieved if we neglect his
kindnesses, ignoring his many revelations and
invitation to join the banquet? When we to face him,
what excuse can we make?

> *"For what can be known about God is plain to them,
> because God has shown it to them. For his invisible
> attributes, namely, his eternal power and divine nature
> have been clearly perceived, ever since the creation of
> the world, in the things that have been made. So they
> are without excuse." (Romans 1:19,20)*

We are made to seek and find God, but I'm not saying
it is easy to find God. Things get confusing. Our own
ignorance makes the road difficult. We are presented
with many other paths. We have many ideas about who
God is – or if He is. This can't be helped. Jesus knows
we are lost and in need of help. Walking among us,
he looked past our faults, offering to help guide our way
to God:

> *"And Jesus went throughout all the cities and villages,
> teaching in their synagogues and proclaiming the gospel
> of the kingdom and healing every disease and every
> affliction. When he saw the crowds, he had compassion*

for them, because they were harassed and helpless, like sheep without a shepherd." (Matthew 9:35-38)

We may get lost on the journey but we have no excuse for failing to seek God until we find him. God is eager to help. We, too, are made to help each other seek out God, *"Seek and you shall find. For the one who seeks shall find." (Matthew 7:7)*

When we enter into God's conversation with us, we are already on the road to finding.

God wants to know each one of us. Getting to know God is not a 'life option' or an elective. It is life's defining purpose. We are made to seek and find. In one sermon, Paul the apostle points his hearers to God. He adds that one day they will give an account for their seeking – or not:

"Since we are his offspring...the times of ignorance God overlooked, but now he commands all people everywhere to repent, because he has fixed a day on which he will judge the world in righteousness by a man whom he has appointed; and of this he has given assurance to all by raising him from the dead." (Acts 17:29-31)

Among all the ways we can make sense of life, and fulfill our purpose and destiny is to enter the search – and to find God.

Of course the main reason to seek is not in order to avoid failure – the reason we set out on a quest is to find. We seek God in order to find him.

The sorrow of missing out in the quest to find God is ultimately tragic. Finding God is the greatest joy a human being can experience.

"In your presence is fullness of joy. In your right hand are pleasures forever more." (Psalm 16:11)

Our ultimate and complete fulfillment consists in knowing God. Jesus explains, *"And this is eternal life, that they know you the only true God, and Jesus Christ whom you have sent." (John 17:3)*

God himself if the reward and joy of the seeking. This is more than being religious. Religion is about God helping a person find a purpose or meaning in life. Christianity is about a man woman or child finding God and knowing him forever.

If you are daunted by the challenge of finding God, or encounter confusion or opposition – there is help for you. From the above, clearly God wants to be found. He is also willing to help. A simple prayer is all that is needed, to open the door to his help:

"You will seek me and you will find me when you seek me with all your heart." (Jeremiah 29:7)

"If my people will humble themselves and pray and seek my face....then I will hear from heaven." (2 Chronicles 7:14)

"Seek the Lord while he may be found, call upon him while he is near." (Isaiah 55:6)

"They that seek me find me." (Proverbs 8:17)

When you get discouraged, confused or sense opposition, Jesus is standing by, ready to help if you ask:

"Come to me, all who labor and are heavy laden, and I will give you rest. Take my yoke upon you, and learn from me, for I am gentle and lowly in heart, and you will find rest for your souls. For my yoke is easy, and my burden is light." (Matthew 11:23,24)

This is the seeker's greatest comfort. Jesus is not indifferent to your needs. His life and death and resurrection are all part of a grand plan to seek and find us. He speaks of his whole life purpose as finding those who seek him.

"The son of man came to seek and save the lost."
(Luke 19:10)

He sums up his mission in life and death as one of finding those who need him:

"If I be lifted up I will draw all men to myself."
(John 12:32)

***

God is in the conversation. Prayer is listening to him speak and inviting him to take us further and deeper. The last three conversations in this book are about prayer – bringing God into the conversation. It seems fitting that we end this exploration of God with a hopefilled prayer. It is a prayer I often pray:

"I urge that supplications, prayers and thanksgivings be made for all people... this is good, and pleasing in the sight of God our Savior, who desires all people to be saved and to come to the knowledge of the truth. For there is one God, and there is one mediator between God and men, the man Christ Jesus, who gave himself as a ransom for all.
(1 Timothy 2:4-6)

Appendix

Bringing God into the Conversation

God conversations are good for the soul. Time after time, I've found it is interesting and creative to talk about God. It's a great way to deepen relationships. Most importantly, God conversations are the chief way many people get to get to know God.

If God is in a conversation, It isn't a technique. Technique bypasses people. If it becomes a technique you can be sure God isn't in the conversation.

If you would know how to bring God into the conversation these suggestions might help you.

1. Love people.

There is no one so disagreeable that you can't value him or her. Each person is made in God's image. (Genesis 1:24-26)

'We must not brood on the wickedness of man, but realize he is God's image bearer. If we cover and obliterate man's faults and consider the beauty and dignity of God's image in him, then we shall be induced to love and embrace him.' (From The Golden Booklet of the Christian Life)

Jesus loves people. When he looks at the 'maddening crowd' he does not despise their need. He looks past their obvious faults.

"He had compassion on them because they were harassed and helpless, like sheep without a shepherd." Matthew 9:35 ff.

2. Expect to make a friend.

Friendship is built one great conversation on another.

Some say, "Don't discuss religion or politics if you want to make friends.' I would say the opposite is true. In order to get to know anyone well you need to know what matters to them most – their core beliefs and convictions. Friendship involves openness. What someone believes or does not believe about God is at the heart of who they are. Real friends talk about their beliefs because what they believe matters to them and matters to the friendship.

3. Put the person first, not their argument.

It's people that are interesting, creative, and precious. Their point of view comes second. Get to know someone – in good time you will get to know what they value and believe. You are not winning an argument; you are helping another person on their journey. You are awakening them to their own uniqueness. You might waken them to God.

4. Discern where God is speaking.

If someone is seeking ultimate truth, God has put this in his or her heart. "God has put eternity into man's heart," wrote Solomon in Ecclesiastes. If someone is searching, you can be sure God is inviting them to the quest.

5. Tell your story; ask for theirs.

You telling your story offends no one. Often they are happy to share theirs. Your story is an invitation and a kind way to encourage them to think and respond.

6. Expect revelations and enlightenment while you converse.

'Revelation' is the English translation of the word 'apocalupto' or apocalypse. It means to pull back the veil and reveal what is hidden. A good conversation opens the door to new vistas of truth, wisdom and knowledge – especially about God.

'Enlightenment' is translated from the Greek <Epiphano>. It means to be surrounded by light. We talk about how 'the light goes on' when a great idea is shared. God conversations often bring enlightenment – the lights go on. You can see it in each other's eyes.

7. Be open about your beliefs and convictions.

A good conversation about God begins by respecting the other person's foundational beliefs. Respect and listening constitutes 'fair play' in any great conversation.

Your convictions of truth are not always evident to the person you converse with. In my case, as a Christian, the axioms of my thoughts come from a theistic worldview.

"Hey that's not fair!" some might argue, "you're using religion." I would say it's only unfair if you deny or hide your beliefs. None of us starts from 'the simple truth.' We all have underlying assumptions and convictions, even if we are no more aware of these than a fish is of the water he swims in.

8. Be informed. Get to know what others believe.

A good conversationalist is a bit of a philosopher. Philosophy means to love knowledge. A philosopher is curious and eager to learn. The alternative is ignorance. Some of the things I have read to deepen my conversations include:

- Thích Nhat Hanh, *The Heart of Buddha's Teaching*
- *Bhagavad Gita*
- *The Koran*
- Writings of Atheists like Voltaire, Nietzsche, Richard Dawkins
- New Age thinkers like Dan Brown
- Scientists like Brian Green
- Defenders of the Christian faith: Blaise Pascal, GK Chesterton, Dorothy Sayers, CS Lewis, Timothy Keller
- Lots of philosophy, several courses at university
- Literature, both classic and contemporary are a great way to discern 'the spirit of the age'
- The Bible. Objectively it is hands down the most formative book of western civilization, and increasingly the rest of the world.

I keep up with science for lay people by reading Scientific American, Discovery and other educational magazines. Brian Green is a great teacher to keep up to date.

As I read, I learn things that delight me. I want to be a lover of learning. As I keep reading I learn more about my own beliefs and am able to converse intelligently about other views.

9. Learn to ask good questions.

A good question has a way of awakening us to the quest. For example, Plato shaped all of his writings in the form of dialogues. These dialogues are filled with probing questions. His aim is to lead his hearers to a purer idea of what is true and what is good.

Jesus takes a similar approach. For example, when he meets a Samaritan woman at the well he takes her from surface matters into a deeper conversation. You can find this dialogue in John 4.

Jesus catches her attention by asking her to draw water from the well for him. This question jars her. Why does he ask her to give him water? He wants to awaken her thirst for deeper truths.

"Everyone who drinks of this water will be thirsty again, but whoever drinks of the water that I will give him will never be thirsty again." (John 4:13-14)

Jesus takes her deeper with another question. He asks to meet her husband. She says, "I have no husband."

Jesus said to her, *"You are right in saying, 'I have no husband'; for you have had five husbands, and the one you now have is not your husband. What you have said is true."* (John 4:17-18)

Jesus goes down the well of her life history to help her search her heart. The woman is awakened to the reality underlying the conversation. She simply has to know who he is:

The woman said to him, "I know that Messiah is coming (he who is called Christ). When he comes, he will tell us all things." Jesus said to her, "I who speak to you am he." (John 4:25-26)

The woman at the well has her thirst satisfied.

10. Pray for appointments.

Someone has said, "When I pray, coincidences happen." I find when I pray for the opportunity to bring God into the conversation, I often find my self in the middle of one. This is no accident. It's an appointment. I get to be God's messenger in Him speaking to someone. What a privilege.

God desires all men to come to a knowledge of the truth. (I Timothy 2:1)

God in the Conversation

Prayer
Current
Navigating Life Through Prayer

Prayer Current helps people navigate life
through prayer. Whether someone is just
entering the waters or is an experienced
traveler, Prayer Current provides
inspiration and practical tools
to grow in prayer, and to
"pray it forward" by helping grow others
in prayer. Designed for life in the city
and for personal or church use,
Prayer Current resources engage people
in a balance of reflection, interaction,
study, actual prayer practice,
and mission.

www.prayercurrent.com

CPSIA information can be obtained at www.ICGtesting.com
Printed in the USA
LVOW10s1240150216

475159LV00001B/1/P